BRIGHT IDEAS
FOR YOUR HOME

BRIGHT IDEAS
FOR YOUR HOME

Per Dalsgaard and Elisabeth Erichsen

Harper & Row, Publishers
New York, Hagerstown, San Francisco, London

CONTENTS

PER   ELISABETH

Per Dalsgaard and Elisabeth Erichsen live in a delightful rambling apartment, largely furnished and decorated with their own designs, in the heart of Copenhagen. They have been there since 1973, but the seed of this book started slightly earlier.

Per used to be a well-known fashion and advertising photographer. In 1970 he wanted a suite of furniture, but furniture was not only too expensive to buy, it was also impossible to find anything he liked. His knowledge of furniture construction was nil, but his enthusiasm was boundless, so he designed exactly the suite he wanted, bought himself an old sewing machine, and started work on the furniture of his fantasies. The results were, in the eyes of his friends and himself, so fantastic that he immediately photographed his creations.

Shortly afterwards, the editor of a big magazine visited Per's apartment on completely other business and was so taken by the furniture and the photographs that he suggested Per should try his designs on the Do-It-Yourself market, which Per did – with immediate success. He had instinctively struck on the right formula. His designs were simple to make, inexpensive, bright, and combined Do-It-Yourself with home decoration.

Since 1973, Per and Elisabeth have been designing, constructing, photographing and selling their ideas for the home to magazines all over the world. Their inspiration has largely come from the things they wanted to make for their own apartment. They make everything themselves, and the prototype is tested and modified until they are satisfied that it can be offered to the public with the assurance that it works, it looks good and it will last.

Their hallmark is a brilliant design sense, using strong bright colors in unusual combinations and settings. So far they have dreamed up more than 70 different Do-It-Yourself series, and they show no signs of flagging.

INTRODUCTION

This is a book of ideas – not a traditional Do-It-Yourself book. It presumes no previous Do-It-Yourself experience, yet it is the first book to combine home decoration with Do-It-Yourself. You could say that it is two books in one.

We have taken great care to arrange all the objects we have made in settings which are not only attractive in themselves but which will give you hundreds of other ideas for transforming your home.

Use and adapt our designs.

You will see from the photographs how all sorts of different ideas suit each other. You may not want a new sofa, but when you look at our photographs of sofas something else may catch your eye and set off a string of new and stimulating thoughts about design and color.

We started to make a lot of our own furniture and other objects when we got our new apartment. What we liked in the shops was too expensive, and anyway most of it did not suit our tastes. So we set about creating exactly what we wanted for a remarkably low cost, and have continued to do so and design all sorts of things for the home ever since.

Our "bright ideas" have more often than not been the results of working out the simplest and the cheapest ways of making things.

The furniture may look expensive and complicated. Well it certainly looks expensive, but it is not difficult to make. And it has two additional advantages, you can be certain that it is not like your neighbor's, and you can easily replace it or add to it.

We have made sure that everything we describe can be made simply, from easily obtainable materials. (We have included a few Hints on page 10–13 on how best to work with the materials.) Everything can be put together with the usual household tools, even in the limited space of a one room apartment.

There is often no right or wrong way or interpreting our ideas. The choice is yours. Choose your materials to suit your pocket and your home. We have often used chipboard and foam rubber in preference to more expensive materials, as long as good looks and serviceability are not sacrificed. Whether you are working within an existing decorative scheme, brightening up here and there, or furnishing a new home, there is no greater pleasure than making real the thing you see in your mind's eye.

Get the whole family to help you. Home is a place that matters, and contributing to it is as enjoyable a family activity as picnics or arguments!

Our best wishes to you and your home.

Per Dalsgaard and Elisabeth Erichsen
Spring 1978

HINTS
ON METHODS AND MATERIALS

Here we have gathered together some hints which will help you when buying materials and when you get down to making the objects in this book. We have used simple symbols throughout the book at the head of each of the 27 sections to give you an idea of what skills are required, so if you are not familiar with some material or method we employ, just refer to these Hints under the relevant symbol.

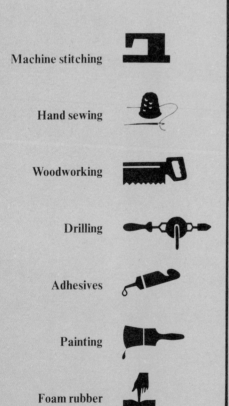

Machine stitching

Hand sewing

Woodworking

Drilling

Adhesives

Painting

Foam rubber

Measurements in this book
Measurements have been carefully worked out, so it is important that you follow the ones we give as accurately as possible.

Exact measurements are given for pieces of wood, chipboard etc, but *when cutting fabric add an extra 1cm (½in) around all pattern pieces* to allow for seams, unless otherwise stated. If you are using a fabric with a large pattern which must match down the seams, make an extra allowance on the length to enable you to get the match absolutely correct.

Use pencil for drawing measurements on wood and chipboard, and tailor's chalk for drawing pattern pieces on fabric.

Fabrics and stitching
Use machine-washable fabrics wherever possible. If you are using loose weave fabrics and intend to wash them later, try to buy them pre-shrunk. You can buy special shampoos for cleaning covers etc. without taking them off.

We have always cut our fabrics *with* the weave, and not on the bias, except on one or two occasions which we have noted in the text.

Make sure your shears are sharp.

Practically all the designs using fabrics can be machine sewn. We have used plain running stitch, but remember to use synthetic sewing thread for synthetic fabrics and cotton thread for natural ones.

Test stitch length and foot pressure on a scrap of fabric before starting to sew in earnest. Thick fabrics obviously need a longer stitch length and lighter foot pressure than thin ones.

Quilting
A quilted panel consists of two pieces of fabric, a top piece and a back piece, with padding or wadding sandwiched between them. These are stitched together through all thicknesses to give a quilted effect. Machine-stitched quilting looks very professional, but mark your intended seam lines with chalk first, then baste along them and pin either side of them to prevent the layers creeping in relation to each other when you start to stitch. Decrease the foot pressure of your machine slightly so that you stretch the panel as little as possible when stitching. Always stitch in the same direction if you can so that any stretching occurs in the same direction.

Appliqué
This simply means sewing a small, usually decorative, piece of fabric to a larger one. Again, baste first to keep it in place before machine stitching. Raw edges can be turned under or hidden with close zig-zag stitching.

Woodworking

If possible, get your supplier to cut all your wood and board to the size we suggest. Then you are just left with the fun of putting it all together. If your supplier cannot cut your wood, use whatever saw you have to hand; but for the best results we have noted below the appropriate saws for the purpose.

Wood

Where wood is used, it is usually softwood (deal). When buying, watch out for warped boards, splits in the ends and inconvenient knots. (To prevent knots weeping, you can apply "knotting", which will be available at your supplier.)

Batten is the term we use for wood lengths of small section.

Dowel is wood of circular section.

Plywood

The most common grade has one nearly perfect side while the other is usually patched. Make sure you use the better side for any finished surface.

Cut plywood with a panel saw. For small pieces, you can use a tenon saw, which will not tear the reverse side so much.

Chipboard

This is made from wood particles bonded together. It is useful for making components which will not show in the finished article. It is cheaper than solid timber and comes in a wide variety of sizes and grades. We have used standard grade throughout.

You can buy special chipboard screws, double threaded along the length of the shank. (Ordinary screws may pull out of chipboard).

Hardboard

Made from wood pulp compressed into sheets, it has a smooth finished side and a coarse textured one. It comes in various thicknesses. You can also buy tempered hardboard, which has been impregnated

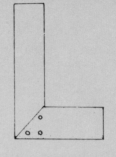

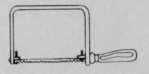

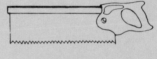

From top to bottom:
Try square
Panel saw
Tenon saw
Coping saw

with oil. We have used this for smartening up dull doors.

Cut hardboard with a panel saw on the face side. If working with an enameled hardboard, score the cutting line first, to prevent the enamel chipping away.

Blockboard

This is usually made of a core of softwood sandwiched between veneers of birch. It can be bought in large sheets, and the veneer provides a handsome finish so that it can be used for table tops. The core is visible on the edges, so these need to be well filled and

sanded or covered with a lipping of softwood.
Cut with a panel saw.

Insulation Board

This includes all sorts of fibre board and makes good bulletin or display board material. It can be cut with a sharp craft knife or with a panel saw.

Useful Tools

A steel rule is quite a good investment, and you can also use it as a straight edge against which to cut with a craft knife.

A try square is ideal for measuring right angles, but if you cannot get one work with a good set square or even the corner of a square-cut board.

Mark rounded corners with the edge of a cup or plate. For larger circles tie one end of a piece of string to a pencil and the other to a thumbtack. Place thumbtack at centre of circle and adjust length of string to give the required radius.

Cutting

A tenon saw gives a good clean straight cut and should be used with a mitre box for all joint cutting. Because it has a stiffening rib along the top of the blade, it cannot be used for cutting wide sheets of chipboard etc.

A panel saw is a good all purpose saw, with more widely spaced teeth than the tenon saw. Always cut to the waste side of your marked line to allow for the width of the cut.

A coping saw is used for cutting curves or cut-out shapes in timber or board. It can only cut into the wood as far as the distance between the back of the saw and the blade, but the angle of the blade can be altered to negotiate tight curves within the distance limitation. When making a cut in the middle of a piece of wood, drill a hole in the waste part of the wood large enough to take the blade. Thread the blade through the hole and then fix it back in the frame. Apply tension to the blade by tightening the handle.

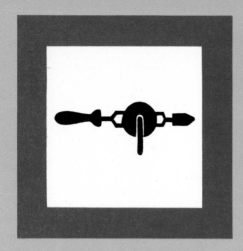

Drilling

For small holes a wheel brace is fine, but for larger ones use a hand brace. An electric drill speeds up the job.

Fixing

The best all-purpose hammer is a claw hammer. If you have to extract nails, use a small piece of wood (an offcut) between the hammer and the good wood to protect the surface when you lever up the nail.

Your screwdriver must fit the slot of the screw you are using. Use a spanner of the right size or an adjustable spanner for tightening bolts.

Use countersunk screws for woodwork. Drill a countersunk hole for the head and screw until the head is below the surface of the wood. Then fill the hole flush with filler.

Use oval nails for woodworking. Hammer them in with the oval in the direction of the grain. Nail thinner piece of timber to thicker and don't over-nail. Where two nails will hold, three may well split the wood. Drive nails in at an angle for added strength.

Panel pins are good for joining small abutted or mitred corners or for joining small pieces of wood. They must be used in conjunction with adhesive.

We occasionally use nuts and bolts on furniture for the stronger constructions. They can be bought with square or hexagonal heads. Ideally washers should be inserted between the head of the bolt and the wood and the nut and the wood to prevent the nut and the bolt head biting into the timber.

Clamps are invaluable–for clamping together glued surfaces and holding together edges that need to be sanded. (Use small pieces of cardboard or hardboard between the clamp's pads to prevent them marking the wood.)

Mitre boxes are not expensive. They hold the timber steady when using a tenon saw and are so constructed that you can make accurate 45° and 90° cuts.

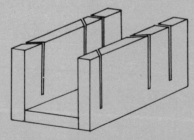

Joining

The simplest corner joint is a butt joint. The two pieces of timber are abutted, glued and screwed or nailed together. To strengthen the butt joint you can put a triangular piece of batten or quadrant in the corner through which you screw or nail into the abutting timber. This ensures good right angle joints and a sound frame. L-shaped metal angle brackets can also be used to strengthen a simple butt joint.

A dowelling joint is used to make a flat butt joint which shows no fixing marks. First cut the ends of the wood square. Clamp the two pieces together and on the edges mark the positions for the holes. Drill holes in these positions a little deeper than half the length of the dowel pegs. (Mark the depth required on the drill with a piece of white tape.) For the pegs use dowel about $\frac{1}{3}$ the thickness of the wood. Sand off the ends of the pegs and cut a groove along the length of each one to allow the excess glue to escape. Put glue into both sets of holes and push the pegs firmly into one board then fit the other board over them. Clamp the two pieces together to keep them abutted while the glue sets.

Mitred corners are best glued and then pinned with panel pins. Knock the pins home at an angle so that they won't pull out.

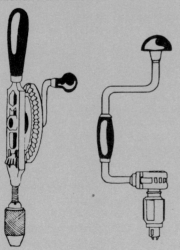

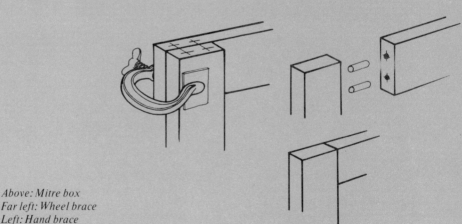

Above: Mitre box
Far left: Wheel brace
Left: Hand brace
Right: Stages in making dowelling joint

Finishing
Follow the manufacturer's instructions carefully for paints, stains etc.

Sanding
Sand all wood surfaces after they have been assembled or before painting or varnishing. Use a sanding block where possible and always sand in the direction of the grain.

Painting
Before painting all wood or board surfaces, seal with primer. Use an undercoat if you like, and then apply one or two top coats of paint. Sand lightly between coats.

Staining
Some stains react with certain varnishes, so if you intend to finish the surface with varnish use a stain recommended by the varnish manufacturer. A water stain will not react with varnish, but it can raise the grain on the wood, so sand after applying.
   Apply stain directly on a sanded surface with a non-fluffy cloth or soft brush and work in the direction of the grain.

Varnishing
Polyurethane varnish gives a good heat and water resistant surface. Clear varnish comes in mat, gloss and satin finishes, and some makes come in colors too. For a really smooth finish, sand before applying each coat.

Adhesives
Follow the manufacturer's instructions carefully.

For gluing timber and board, use a proprietary brand of woodworking adhesive. Most suppliers stock a range of suitable adhesives and are willing to advise.

For jobs involving foam rubber, it is important that you use a natural latex contact adhesive. Other adhesives may react with the foam or simply not bond at all.

When working with cork tiles try to get the contact adhesive specially manufactured for use with cork.

For fabrics most cellulose-based household adhesives will do. Make sure that the one you use dries clear, and if in doubt try it on a small piece of fabric first. Rubber-based adhesives are also good with fabric, since they form a flexible bond.

Before any gluing, make sure that the surfaces are free from dust, dirt and grease, and follow the maker's instructions carefully.

Foam Rubber
A good Do-It-Yourself foam warehouse will stock various densities of foam from very soft to very firm. Standard density (in the range 20-25kg/m^3) will do for all the major furnishing items in this book.

Most warehouses will cut foam to size. For non-rectangular shapes provide the cutter with a full size cardboard template of the piece you want, and specify the thickness. (If you are quite unable to get the foam cut professionally, you can cut smaller pieces with a fine toothed hacksaw blade, but the results will not be very good.) Thin sheets of foam can be cut with shears.

Use a natural latex contact adhesive for bonding.

Foam rubber chips are little pieces of foam of all grades and colors used for stuffing cushions. Zippered closures in the cushion covers enable you to plump up the stuffing from time to time. Foam rubber chips are not washable (the dye in the foam runs), but they can be dry cleaned.

List of sources of materials

For the most part, your local lumber yard, hardware, fabric or variety store will be able to supply you with the materials needed to complete projects described in this book.

The following are sources of mail-order household equipment which will supply catalogs on request.

J.C. Penney Inc.
1301 Ave. of the Americas
New York, N.Y. 10019

Sears, Roebuck & Co.
Dept. 139-CHC
4640 Roosevelt Blvd.
Philadelphia, Pa. 19132

Montgomery Ward
Dept. CHC
Montgomery Ward Plaza
Chicago, Ill. 60681

TABLES, CHAIRS & SOFAS

This is a refreshing, go-anywhere, do-anything sectional furniture design. As you'll see from the photographs, the Checky Charlie sections can be arranged in all sorts of ways to suit any shape of room. And we've made them only 75 × 75cm (30 × 30in) so that they can be used even in the smaller rooms, such as a hallway or a study.

The three basic units–chair, corner chair and table–are constructed in the same way, with slight modifications. The beauty of Checky Charlie is that it makes the best of a beautiful natural material, pine wood. Because the design is simple, only basic skills, and a good measure of precision, are needed to produce very professional looking results.

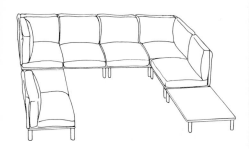

Materials needed

For each basic unit (chair or table)

Wood:

 4 pieces 75 × 7 × 3cm (30 × 3 × 1¼in)

 4 pieces 61 × 1.5 × 1.5cm
  (24 × ⅝ × ⅝in) for inner frame

 4 pieces 1cm (⅜in) dowel 7cm (2¾in)
  long for pegging legs

 Plywood 6mm (¼in) thick: 61 × 61cm
  (24 × 24in)

Drill with 4.2cm (1¾in) flat bit

Wood adhesive, panel pins, polyurethane
 varnish

File, coarse and fine glasspaper

For table (in addition to materials for
the basic unit)

Wooden dowel 4.2cm (1¾in) diameter
 for legs: 4 pieces 27cm (11in) long

Glass at least 5mm thick: 61 × 61cm
 (24 × 24in) for top

Fabric (optional): 70 × 70cm
 (28 × 28in)

For chair (in addition to materials for
the basic unit)

Wooden dowel 4.2cm (1¾in) diameter
 for legs: 2 pieces 27cm (11in) long
 2 pieces 65cm (26in) long

Canvas for backrest: 58 × 104cm
 (23 × 41in)

Cushion fabric: 2.80m–90cm wide
 (3yd–36in) or 2m–120cm wide
 (2¼yd–48in); same for inner cover if
 required

Zippers: two 70cm (28in) long for outer
 covers
 two 25cm (10in) long for inner covers

Foam rubber chips

For corner chair (in addition to
materials for the basic unit)

Wooden dowel 4.2cm (1¾in) diameter
 for legs: 1 piece 27cm (11in) long
 3 pieces 65cm (26in) long

Canvas for backrest:
 1 piece 58 × 208cm (23 × 82in)
 1 piece 42 × 22cm (17 × 9in) for
  centre panel

Cushion fabric: 3.50m–90cm wide
 (4yd–36in) or 2.60m–120cm wide
 (2⅞yd–48in); same for inner cover if
 required

Zippers: two 65cm (26in) and one 60cm
 (24in) long for outer covers three
 25cm (10in) long for inner covers

Foam rubber chips

Making the chair or table frame

Saw a square of wood 1.5cm ($\frac{5}{8}$in) thick off both ends of the four 75cm (30in) lengths of wood and stick the four lengths together as illustrated in **Fig 1**. When the adhesive is thoroughly dry stick and pin the four 1.5 × 1.5cm ($\frac{5}{8} \times \frac{5}{8}$in) lengths of wood (mitred at each end), to the inside of the frame, flush with its lower surface (**Fig 2**). The holes which take the four legs are drilled with a flat bit 4.2cm ($1\frac{3}{4}$in) in diameter. Centre each hole as shown in the upper diagram in **Fig 2**.

Now drill a hole exactly 1cm ($\frac{3}{8}$in) in diameter exactly through the diameter and exactly 24cm ($9\frac{3}{4}$in) from one end of each dowel leg (**Fig 3**). These are the holes which take the 1cm ($\frac{3}{8}$in) dowel pegs on which the frame rests. The top of each short leg is flush with the top of the frame once its peg is in place. Use

adhesive to stop the short legs turning. The longer legs which make the chair back are left loose in their holes.

Using a file and glasspaper round off all the edges and corners which will be visible in the finished article. Sand all surfaces smooth and finish with a coat or two of polyurethane varnish.

Finally, put the panel of plywood, plain for the chair or covered with fabric for the table, into its recess (**Fig 4**). The sheet of glass goes in next if you are making the table. (Take the plywood to your glazier so that the glass can be cut to exactly the same size.)

Making the chair backrest

The backrest for the ordinary chair is made as follows. Turn all the edges of the 58 × 104cm (23 × 41in) rectangle of canvas under by 1 cm ($\frac{1}{2}$in) and baste. Now turn the two longer edges under again by 11 and 5cm (4 and 2in) respectively and the shorter edges by 14cm ($5\frac{1}{2}$in) and stitch them down–as if they were wide hems. You should now have a piece of canvas 74cm (29in) wide by 40cm (16in) high (**Fig 5**). Run a line of stitching across the top to prevent the backrest slipping down the poles. Now slip the canvas over the poles and see how close to the poles your final lines of stitching should be.

The backrest for the corner chair is made in the same way but has an extra panel (as can be seen in **Fig 5**) stitched to it to take the center pole. Turn the edges of the panel 1cm ($\frac{1}{2}$in) under all round before stitching it in position.

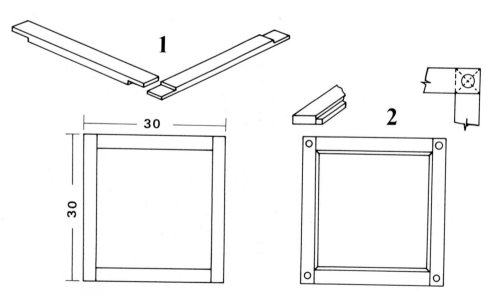

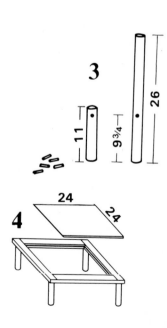

Making the cushions

As you can see from the photographs we economized on fabric by making only the cushion tops/fronts in checkered fabric.

Each cushion consists of two rectangles and a long 10cm (4in) wide strip of fabric which goes round the outside. **Fig 5** shows the *finished* dimensions of all the cushions. Here we list the sizes of the fabric pieces needed to make them up (1cm ($\frac{1}{2}$in) seam allowance throughout):

Cushion A
   2 pieces 78 × 38cm (31$\frac{1}{2}$ × 15$\frac{1}{2}$in)
   1 piece 10 × 232cm (4 × 94in)
Cushion B
   2 pieces 78 × 72cm (31$\frac{1}{2}$ × 29in)
   1 piece 10 × 300cm (4 × 121in)
Cushion C
   2 pieces 72 × 38cm (29 × 15$\frac{1}{2}$in)
   1 piece 10 × 220cm (4 × 89in)
Cushion D
   2 pieces 72 × 72cm (29 × 29in)
   1 piece 10 × 288cm (4 × 116in)
Cushion E
   2 pieces 64 × 38cm (26 × 15$\frac{1}{2}$in)
   1 piece 10 × 204cm (4 × 83in)

Longer zippers are allowed for the outer than for the inner cushion covers. In all cases the bottom back seam is the best place to insert the zipper.

Be generous with the foam filling, making the seat cushions firmer than the back cushions.

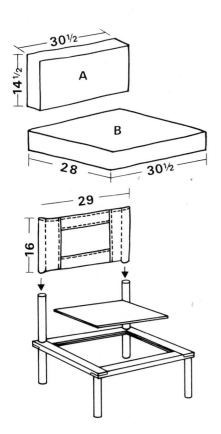

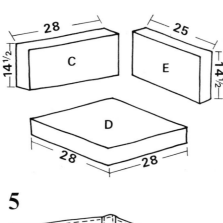

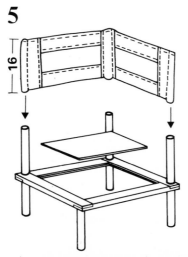

5

BLUE HEAVEN

We designed this sectional suite for its comfort and its looks. It is so straightforward to make that you can run up a Blue Heaven chair in an evening. There is no woodwork to worry about. All you need are the materials, a sewing machine and a tin of contact glue. Your supplier will cut the plywood to size, but you do not even need plywood, if your chair backs on to a wall.

We used a blue velveteen for the covers, but a fabric of similar weight–a heavy rep, cord velvet, perhaps even a good thick upholstery cotton–would be just as suitable.

Materials
Foam rubber block:
  70 × 40 × 20cm (28 × 16 × 8in)
Foam rubber block:
  70 × 85 × 25cm (28 × 33 × 10in)
Foam rubber pad:
  66 × 33 × 2.5cm (26 × 13 × 1in)
Foam rubber chips
Fabric:
  max. 6.30m–120cm wide (7yd–48in)
  or 7.20m–90cm wide (8yd–36in)
6mm plywood: 68 × 63cm (27 × 25in)
Contact glue

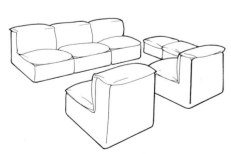

Making the chair

Stick the foam rubber blocks together to make the L-shaped chair shown in **Fig 1** (see also photographs). Center the piece of plywood on the back of the chair and stick in position.

The chair cover is made up in three pieces–one long piece (X) to cover the back, top, front and seat, plus two L-shaped side pieces (Y in **Fig 2**). Cut one piece X and two Y pieces (one reversed), referring to **Fig 2** for dimensions. Allow an extra 1cm ($\frac{1}{2}$in) on all seams. Note the tapered flaps along the base edges which are used to secure the cover underneath the chair. Pin, tack and stitch the L-shapes to piece X matching points ABCDEF. Extend the seam slightly past A and F so that the cover will fit around the chair's bottom corners.

Turn the chair upside down and using a sharp knife make four slits in the foam rubber base. The slits should be about 8cm (3in) deep and will hold the tapered flaps on the bottom of the chair cover. Turn the cover right side out, hem the bottom raw edges, and slip over the chair. Pull the flaps round the bottom edges of the chair and push them firmly into the slits so that the cover is held taut over the chair (see photograph and **Fig. 3**).

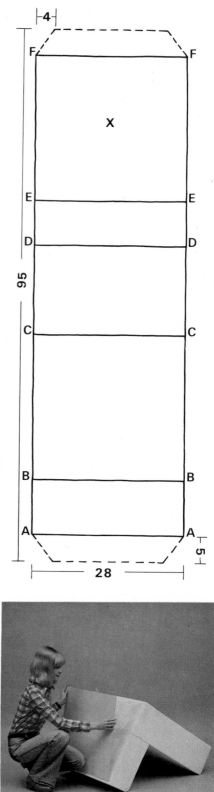

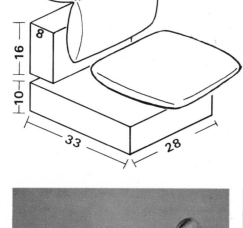

Making the chair cushions

For each chair, the cushions consist of a head and back cushion made in one and a separate seat cushion.

For the seat cushion cut two pieces of fabric as shown in **Fig 4,** left (allowing an extra 1cm (½in) on the seams). Stitch them together right sides facing, leaving an opening in the seam to take the foam filling. Turn them right side out. Fill the cushion quite firmly with the chips, then stitch the opening closed.

For the head and back cushion, cut two pieces of fabric as shown in **Fig 4,** right (allowing 1cm (½in) on seams). Stitch them together right sides facing, leaving two openings of 25cm (10in) for filling, one on each of the longer sides. Turn the cover right side out. Measure 38cm (15in) along one of the 68cm (27in) sides and run a line of stitching across the width of the cover. This divides the cushion into a 38cm (15in) back cushion and a 30cm (12in) head cushion.

Now loosely fill the head cushion with foam and sew the opening closed. Before you fill the back cushion, slip in the pad of 2.5cm (1in) thick foam and put the chip filling on top of that. (The foam sheet will keep the back cushion upright.) Sew the opening closed, plump the cushions well and arrange on the chair.

BLUE HEAVEN STOOL

Making the stool and cushion

Make up a cover for the stool on the same lines as the chair cover, allowing for similar base flaps and making the finished cover size slightly smaller than the overall dimensions of the foam block.

The cushion is made exactly the same size as the chair seat cushion.

Materials needed
Foam rubber block:
  25 × 70 × 65cm (10 × 28 × 25in)
Fabric for cover and cushion:
  approx. 3.10m–120cm wide
  (3½yd–48in) or 3.80m–90cm wide
  (4¼yd–36in)
Foam rubber chips

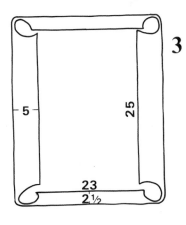

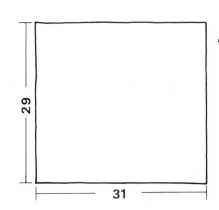

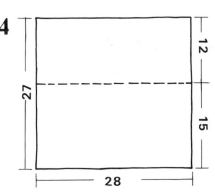

SLUMPER

Here's comfort with the minimum of bother. Even a child of ten could sew it up. In canvas the Slumper could be a garden or patio lounger; in cotton or fake fur a perfect furnishing for a child's room. In deep pile corduroy a seductive, and cheap, alternative to the traditional easy chair. No matter how boldly or subtly the design is interpreted the Slumper says relax, unbend, make friends.

It's a giant cushion really but it gives more support than a conventional floor cushion. Remember that the material you use, wipeable or washable, must be tough enough to stand up to a certain amount of dragging, stretching and pummeling.

Materials needed

Inner cover fabric:
    4m–120cm wide (4½yd–48in) or
    4m–90cm wide (4½yd–36in)
Outer cover fabric: as for inner cover
Zippers:
    one 40cm (16in) long for inner cover
    two 60cm (24in) long for outer cover
Foam rubber chips: 7kg (15lb)
The Slumper has a foam-filled inner
    cushion and zippered cover.

The pattern for the cushion couldn't be simpler—bottom, front and back are all in one piece, with two triangular pieces for the sides. You could of course use a stronger fabric for the bottom piece to give it extra durability. Use ticking or some other cheap but stout, close-woven cotton fabric for the inner cover. This has a short zipper to allow you to add or remove stuffing. The outer cover has a zipper closure 120cm (48in) long. (Zippers of this length are not easy to come by so use two 60cm (24in) zippers instead—they should meet in the middle of the closure.)

To save time we cut out both sets of covers at the same time. Place the outer cover fabric, right side up, exactly on top of the inner cover fabric and pin them together at intervals. Now you can treat them as a single fabric. Following the measurements given in **Fig 1,** which include 1cm (½in) seam allowances, cut out the long piece for the front, back and bottom and then the two triangular side pieces (cut them as a square, then divide diagonally).

Have a good look at **Fig 2** before you start to stitch. Both the inner and outer cushion covers are made in the same way. Seam the side pieces to the bottom first, but for the outer cover remember to leave the last 20cm (8in) of both seams open to take the zipper(s). Now seam the front and back edges of the side pieces to the corresponding edges of the seat. The zippers go in the bottom back seams. In the outer cover they extend a short way along the bottom side seams.

Stuff the inner cushion fairly tight to start with. See how it feels when you sit on it. It should be supportive but soft enough to give comfortably in all the right places. Make sure you poke the inner cushion snugly into the corners of the outer cover.

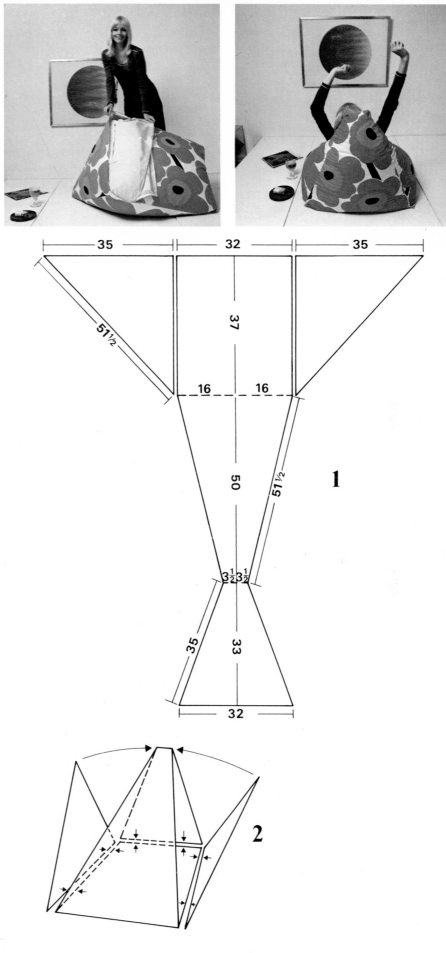

29

'SIDE ONE' CHAIR

Here is a really appealing idea for the young–a low, sturdy, informal, lounging-about chair which can be made in next to no time. Its side profile is that of a figure 1–'Side One'–very eye-catching and unusual. A sewing machine, some fabric and some blocks of foam are all you need. There are no inner covers to bother about, but choose a thickish, good-tempered fabric for the cover–perhaps a heavy cotton, corduroy or tweed or you could make it up in patchwork.

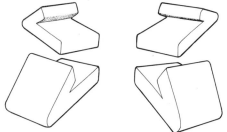

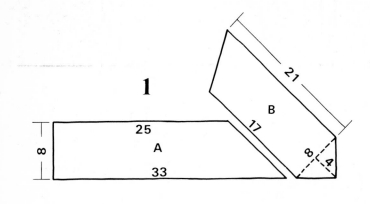

1

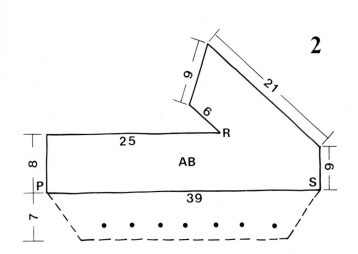

2

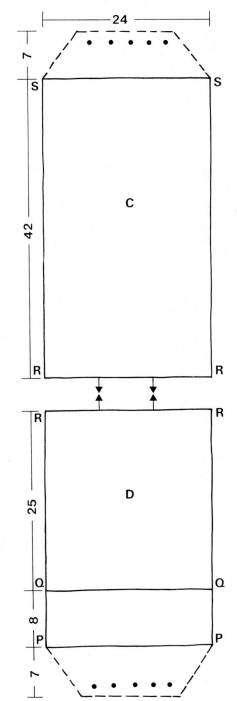

Materials needed for one chair

Foam blocks:
  one 60 × 20 × approx. 90cm for seat
    (A) (24 × 8 × approx. 36in)
  one 60 × 20 × approx. 70cm for back
    (B) (24 × 8 × approx. 28in)
Contact adhesive
Fabric:
  4.50m–90cm wide (5yd–36in) or
    2.70m–120cm wide (3yd–48in)
Large eyelets (approx. 25)
  15m (16½yd) twine or tape

Making the chair

Have the foam blocks cut by an expert.
Ask him to cut them to the sizes given
above first, and provide him with a full
size cardboard template of A and B
(**Fig 1**) so that he can reduce them to
the correct shape.

Stick the blocks together as shown in
the photographs.

The cover has four pieces, two AB
pieces (one reversed), one C, one D
(**Fig 2**). Use the template to help you
cut out the two side pieces (AB) but
remember to add the flap allowance
along the bottom. (You can, of course,
join smaller pieces of material if the

seam is in an inconspicious place.) All
the dimensions given in **Fig 2** include a
1cm (½in) seam allowance.

Join C to D along R, then tack and
seam the side pieces in position
matching the letters P, Q, R and S and
taking the seams only as far as P and S.
Now hem the free edges of the flaps,
making a rather wide hem
(2.5cm–1in–, say) along their long
edges to accommodate the eyelets.
You'll need about seven eyelets along
the longer edges and five along the
shorter. Either cut the corners of the
flaps diagonally or fold them under.
Now comes the most satisfying part!
Ease the cover over the foam blocks
and lace it underneath with twine or
tape.

STUDIO CHAIR

There is immense satisfaction in making something which looks expensive but isn't. The Studio Chair has a classical, elegant design, and it is straightforward to make. Start with one chair and you have the nucleus of a bright and cheerful suite. To make the sofa, simply extend the width of the seat and back by any length you like.

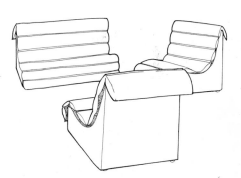

Making and covering the box frame

Draw the pattern for the chair side (A in **Fig 1**) on cardboard first, cut it out and draw the shape of the curve on to your two 76 × 70cm (30 × 28in) pieces of chipboard. Use a coping saw to cut the curves. Sand all edges before assembling.

D in **Fig 1** shows how the pieces are put together–box fashion, with the four square-cross-section wooden blocks at the corners. Use wood adhesive and nails throughout. Attach the four castors to the blocks.

The box frame can now be painted (sand and prime it first) or covered with fabric. Stretch the fabric well over the frame, turn the edges to the inside and stick them down. Neatly oversew any seams in the fabric, making sure they coincide with a corner, preferably a back corner

Fitting the webbing

Measure the curve of the chair side with a tape measure–it should be approximately 110cm (43in). When in position the webbing should have a similar curvature. Simply fasten the webbing, woven as shown in **Fig 2**, to the top surface of the back, front and sides of the box with adhesive and upholstery tacks. Make sure that you don't tighten it. We found the cheapest quality webbing quite strong enough.

Materials needed for the box frame

Chipboard (16mm–½in–thick):
  2 pieces 76 × 70cm (30 × 28in) for sides (A)
  piece 67 × 70cm (26 × 28in) for back (B)
  piece 67 × 22cm (26 × 9in) for front (C)
Wood: 4 pieces 15 × 3.5 × 3.5cm (6 × 1½ × 1½in) for inside corners
4 castors
Webbing: approx. 8.50m–7cm (9½yd–3in) wide
Nails, upholstery tacks, wood adhesive
Tough fabric: 3m–90cm wide (3½yd–36in) or 2.30m–120cm wide (2½yd–48in) to cover box frame or chipboard primer and paint

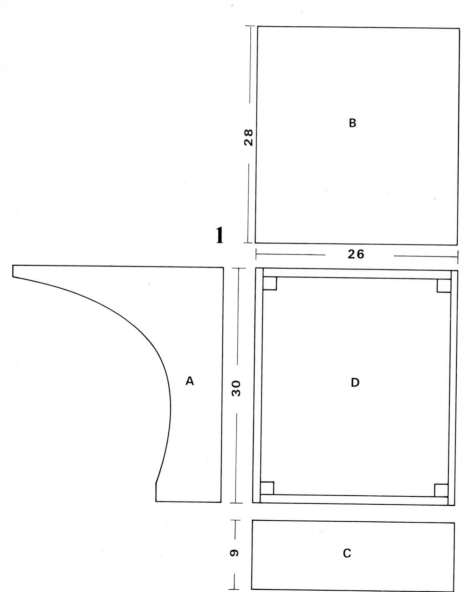

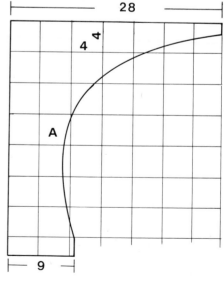

Materials needed for cushion

3.80m fabric–90cm wide (4¼yd–36in wide)
Foam rubber chips

Making the cushion

You could economize here by making the reverse of the cushion in a cheaper fabric. Or you might find it cheaper to use *1.80m of 120cm wide fabric (2yd–48in)*, and let in a panel of calico or canvas at the back. This is a method we used, as you can see from the photograph. Whatever solution you choose, the cushion should be 1.75m (69in) long and 80cm (32in) wide when ready to be filled with the foam chips. Distribute the foam evenly inside it, with slightly less at both ends so that they flop comfortably over the front and back of the chair when you have finished.

Oversew the opening. Starting 19cm (7½in) from the end which will hang over the front of the chair, mark and tack where the rows of quilting will come. There should be eight rows 19cm (7½in) apart, then a 4cm (1½in) gap and a final row 19cm (7½in) from the head end. Ensure there is as little stuffing as possible in the 4cm (1½in) gap.

Now center the cushion on the webbing so that the flat 4cm (1½in) strip rests along the top of the back.

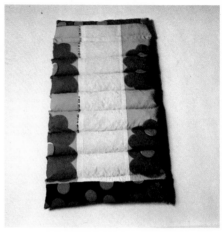

Making a sofa

Simply extend the width of the back and front chipboard panels as desired–the side panels stay the same of course. If you want a very long sofa you will have to brace the frame in the middle (using chipboard and more wood blocks). The finished dimensions of the cushion, before filling and quilting, would have to be 1.75m (69in) long by 80cm (32in) plus the width of your extension.

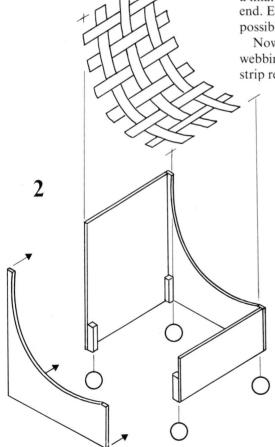

2

At the pace we live today Spring, traditionally the time we start to think about redecorating, is never far away. Could this be the time to change your furniture too? Creating a total new look for a room is as exhilarating as Spring itself.

These Checkmate Chairs are really mini-sofas, two chairs for the price and the effort of one. Push two of them together and you have a party size sofa. Disguised beneath their close fitting checkered covers are sturdy chipboard boxes and blocks of foam. There are no zippers and only one set of covers to sew.

Our red and white chessboard theme called for equally exciting treatment of the walls and drapes. As you can see in the photographs, the white wainscoting continues as a wide white band at the bottom of the drapes.

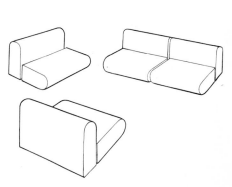

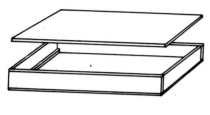

1

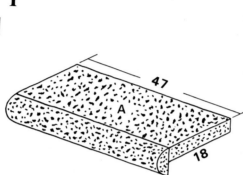

2

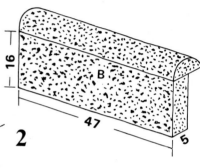

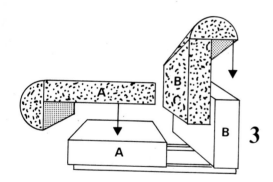

3

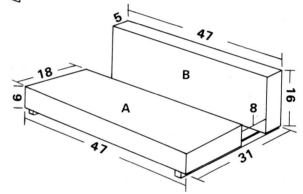

4

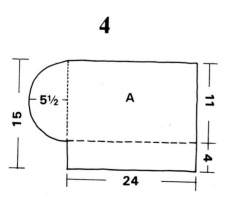

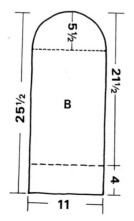

5

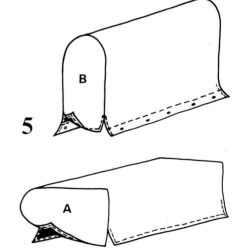

Materials needed for one Checkmate Chair

Chipboard 12mm (½in) thick:

Seat box (A)
  *2 panels 46 × 120cm (18 × 47in) for
    top and bottom*
  *2 panels 13 × 120cm (5 × 47in) for
    long sides*
  *2 panels 13 × 43.5cm (5 × 17in) for
    short sides*

Back box (B)
  *2 panels 40 × 120cm (16 × 47in) for
    front and back*
  *2 panels 10.5 × 120cm (4 × 47in) for
    long sides*
  *2 panels 10.5 × 37.5cm (4 × 15in) for
    short sides*

Wood:
  *two pieces 4.5 × 4.5cm (2 × 2in) and
    43.5cm (17in) long to strengthen
    seat box*
  *two pieces 4.5 × 4.5cm (2 × 2in) and
    37.5cm (15in) long to strengthen
    back box*
  *two pieces 4.5 × 4.5cm (2 × 2in) and
    78cm (31in) long as base supports*

*Wood adhesive, panel pins, nuts and
  bolts with washers*

Foam rubber:
  *1 block 120 × 46 × 10cm
    (47 × 18 × 4in) for seat (A)*
  *1 block 120 × 40 × 12.5cm
    (47 × 16 × 5in) for back (B)*
  *2 half-cylinder blocks 25.5cm (10in)
    diameter × 120cm (47in) long for
    seat front and back top*

Contact adhesive

Cover fabric: 5yd–48in wide or
  3.80m–140cm wide (4⅛yd–54in)*

Large eyelets

Upholstery tacks, twine

**Make sure the fabric does measure
  48in and not 120cm in this case*

Making a Checkmate Chair

The seat box (A) and the back box (B) are both constructed as shown in **Fig 1**, using adhesive and panel pins. Use the 43.5cm (17in) and 37.5cm (15in) battens positioned as in **Fig 1** at each end of the seat and back boxes to strengthen them. Screw the adjoining panels on to them. **Fig 2** shows the finished dimensions of both boxes. Leave the top panel off A and the back panel off B for the time being.

Bolt the two 78cm (31in) lengths of wood to the base of A and B as shown in **Fig 2,** using washers between the nuts and the chipboard and also two washers between the chipboard and the wood to enable you to ease the hems of the cover between them later. As you can see from the photograph (far left) these wooden runners are positioned approximately 12cm (5in) from the edges of the boxes and are bolted flush with the back edges of the back box. They also finish 1cm (½in) from the front edge of the seat box. In other words there should be a 20cm (8in) gap between the boxes. Now stick and pin the missing chipboard panels in position.

The two half-cylinders of foam (cut down from a cylinder of foam 25.5cm (10in) in diameter and 120cm (47in) long) form the front edge of the seat and the top edge of the back. Stick one to foam block A and the other to foam block B as shown in **Fig 2.** Now place the blocks on their respective boxes (**Fig 3**).

The fabric cover should fit very closely over both box/foam units. Be as accurate as possible in cutting the pattern pieces for the sides (A and B in **Fig 4**). These include precisely 1cm (½in) seam allowance all round. For the seat cover you will need two A pieces and a rectangle of fabric 137 × 122cm (54½ × 48in). All three pieces include 10cm (4in) allowances for the flaps which turn under the seat. The back cover will require two B pieces and a slightly longer rectangle of fabric 163.5 × 122cm (65 × 48in). The B piece includes a turn-under of 10cm (4in) and the rectangle a turn-under of 20cm (8in) at both ends.

As you can see from **Fig 5,** which shows both covers made up, the hems around the bottom flaps of the seat cover are fairly narrow. So are those around the shorter bottom flaps of the back cover. But the longer bottom flaps of the latter have a wider hem to accommodate the eyelets.

Clip all curved seams. For extra strength you could also top stitch all seams (**Fig 6**).

Now pull both covers over their respective supports. Ease and smooth the fabric until they are a snug, tight fit. Lace the long flaps of the back cover together with twine, carefully working the flaps under the wooden runners, and tack the other flaps down with upholstery tacks.

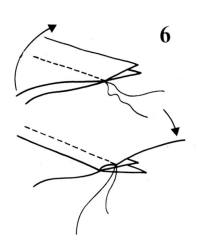

6

In five minutes you can completely re-landscape your living space, with sofas long or short, chairs with or without armrests, and tables low, high or multistoried. All this is possible with four basic types of box unit.

A sofa can be converted into chairs simply by moving the box units. Armrests and base boxes can be used as additional tables. Base boxes can be put into service for your TV or stereo set. Different sized tables can be placed together to produce an interesting stepped table. The variations are endless. Why not start with a chair wide enough for two, with or without armrests?

A hard-wearing hemp fabric is a good cheap covering for the cushions. Wash it before you make them up or they'll shrink to minicushions! And another tip: beat the cushions with a carpet beater to keep them nice and plump.

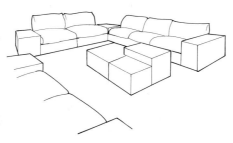

Materials needed for the box units

Chipboard 10mm ($\frac{3}{8}$in) thick cut to the following sizes:

Base box and backboard (A)
  1 panel 80 × 80cm (32 × 32in) for top
  4 panels 79 × 15cm (31$\frac{1}{2}$ × 6in) for sides
  1 panel 60 × 80cm (24 × 32in) for backboard
Armrest (B)
  1 panel 30 × 80cm (12 × 32in) for top
  2 panels 45 × 80cm (18 × 32in) for sides
  2 panels 45 × 28cm (18 × 11in) for ends
Table box (C)
  1 panel 40 × 40cm (16 × 16in) for top
  4 panels 39 × 30cm (15$\frac{1}{2}$ × 12in) for sides
Table box (D)
  1 panel 40 × 40cm (16 × 16in) for top
  4 panels 40 × 39cm (16 × 15$\frac{1}{2}$in) for sides
Wood adhesive, panel, pins, chipboard screws, sandpaper
Chipboard primer, paint and polyurethane varnish or just polyurethane varnish

Making the boxes

Use wood adhesive and panel pins to assemble each unit (**Fig 1**).

Sand the chipboard, especially any sawn edges, as smooth as possible before painting or varnishing. Prime before painting. The backboard should not be screwed to the back panel of the base box until you have finished painting and varnishing.

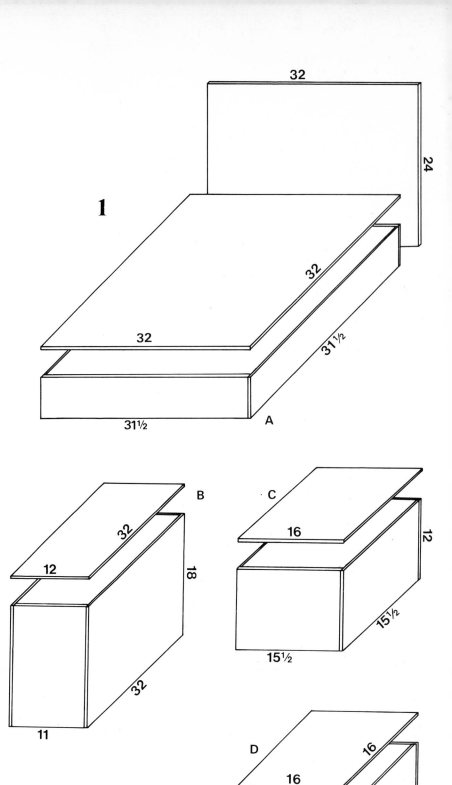

Materials needed for one pair of cushions

Cover fabric: 4m—90cm wide (4½yd— 36in wide) or 3.10m–120cm wide (3½yd–48in)

Zippers for cover: one 75cm (30in) long for back cushion and two 65cm (26in) long for seat cushion

Foam rubber block: 80 × 80 × 10cm (32 × 32 × 4in) for seat

Foam rubber chips

Foam rubber pad: approx. 60 × 60 × 0.5cm (24 × 24 × ¼in)

Making the cushions

Both cushion covers consist of two side pieces (G and H in **Fig 2**) and a rectangle (F for the seat cushion, and E for the back cushion). Remember to *add* a 1cm (½in) seam allowance to all measurements.

As shown in **Fig 3**, the seat cushion is half foam block and half foam chips, but the back cushion is filled with chips only. Both should be stuffed fairly tightly.

The zippers should be included in the back bottom seam of both cushions. The two 65cm (26in) zippers in the seat cover meet in the centre of the back seam. They extend a short way round the bottom seams too.

The seat cushion rests on the foam rubber mat to prevent it slipping.

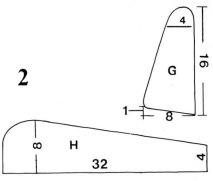

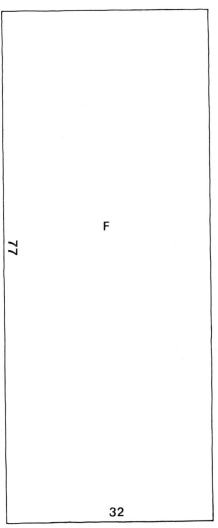

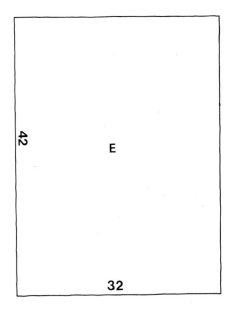

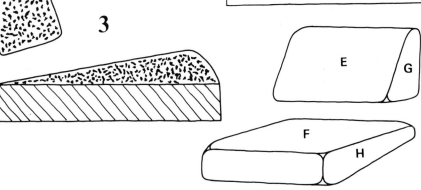

UPHOLSTERED SUITE

Upholstery may sound intimidating. It needn't be. We have been experimenting with the upholstered look for a long time with the aim of producing chunky, modern furniture which uses every possible short cut and relies on non-specialist skills.

Here is a design which answers today's nostalgia for snugness and solidity. We chose a romantic floral fabric for the covers, but abstract prints or plain white would look just as attractive.

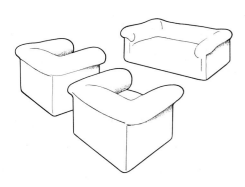

Materials needed for the chair frame

Chipboard:
  *2 panels 81 × 60cm (32 × 24in) for
    sides (A)*
  *1 panel 78 × 60cm (31 × 24in) for
    back (B)*
  *1 panel 78 × 21cm (31 × 8in) for front
    (C)*
Wood 3.5 × 6cm (1½ × 2½in):
  *2 pieces 78cm (31in) long for frame
    (D)*
  *2 pieces 71cm (28in) long for frame
    (D)*
Webbing
*About 14 heavy duty angle brackets
  approx. 6.5cm (2½in) long, 2cm (¾in)
  wide*
Nuts and bolts to fit angle brackets
Wood screws, upholstery tacks
Wood adhesive

Making the chair frame

Use a coping saw to cut the side, back and front panels to shape (**Fig 1**). We suggest that you make a cardboard template for the sides (A) and for the base cutout of B and C so that you end up with the curves matching.

The seat frame (D in **Fig 1** and **Fig 2**) is put together with wood adhesive and screws. Its finished outer dimensions are 78 × 78cm (31 × 31in). Stretch strips of webbing, five one way and four the other, across the frame (**Fig 2**), doubling the ends of the strips under

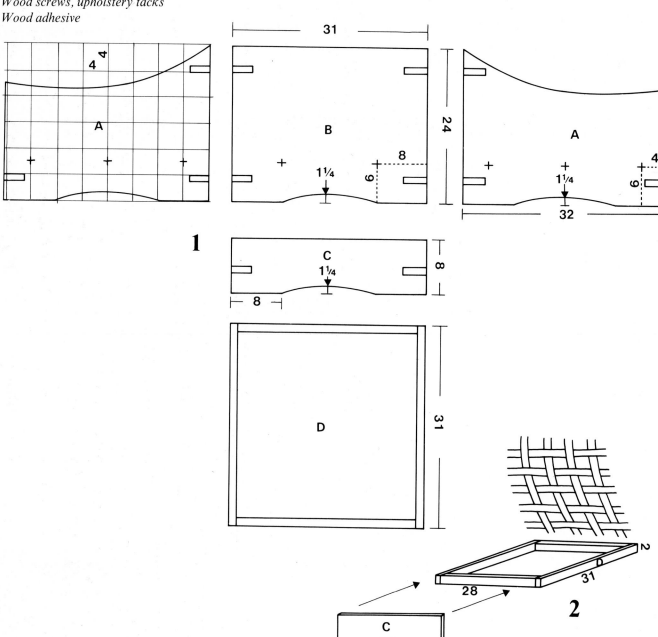

and hammering them down with upholstery tacks. Use a wooden batten as shown in the photograph (opposite top left) to stretch the webbing really tight. Now glue and screw the front panel (C) to the seat frame.

The chair is now assembled using angle brackets and nuts and bolts. Bolt the sides to the back first (angle bracket positions are indicated in **Fig 1**). The angle brackets which support the seat are shown as crosses in **Fig 1** and should be positioned on a line 15cm (6in) from the base of the back and sides. Lastly slide the seat frame and front panel into place, bolt the front panel to the sides with angle brackets (positions marked in **Fig 1** again), and screw the underside of the seat frame to the brackets supporting it.

Now take the chair apart! There is no need to remove the angle brackets which support the seat frame. Just remove the brackets holding the front, sides and back of the chair together, but leave the bolts in position.

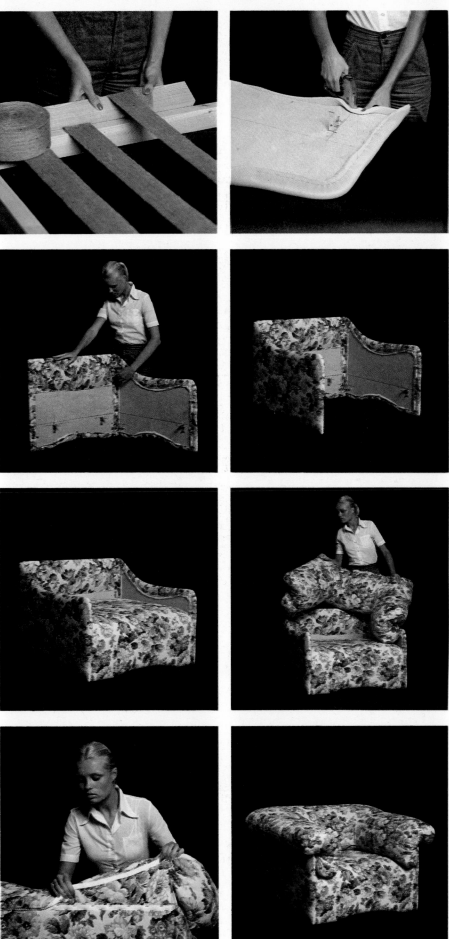

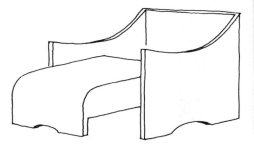

Materials needed for chair upholstery

Staple gun

Foam rubber block: 78 × 68 × 15cm (31 × 27 × 6in) for seat

Foam rubber ¼-cylinder: radius 15cm (6in), length 78cm (31in), for seat edge

Contact adhesive

Foam rubber pad 1.5cm (¾in) thick: approx. 5.50m–120cm wide (6yd–48in)

Fabric: 8m–120cm wide (8¾yd–48in) –cushion alone takes 3.50m (4yd)

Zippers: one 60cm (24in) long

Velcro: 75cm (30in)

Foam rubber chips: 5kg (11lb)

Upholstering the chair

The staple gun is a marvellous timesaver here.

Step 1 is to cover the outside of the back and side panels with a layer of foam rubber 1.5cm (¾in) thick and secure it with staples. We allowed a turnover of about 25cm (10in) at the top of the back panel, as you can see from the photographs on page 49. Work the ends of the bolts through the foam as you go.

The all-in-one seat and front can be covered in the same way, once you have stuck the two foam blocks E and F together and placed them on the seat (**Fig 3**). Use a single large piece of foam to cover the seat and front. Again, work the bolt ends through the foam.

Step 2 is to repeat the covering operation with fabric. Press the bolt ends through small holes made in the fabric as you go. Trim away any excess foam and fabric. Reassemble the chair as before, screwing the seat frame to the supporting brackets.

Step 3 is to make the cushion. **Fig 4** shows the dimensions, which include 1cm (½in) seam allowances, of the five pattern pieces. All except E, the arm end, should be cut on folds, although it would not matter if you cut two B's and two C's (leaving an additional seam allowance) and joined them in the middle, because the seams will hardly show when the cushion is finished and in position.

Put the cushion covers together as illustrated in **Fig 5,** but with right sides inside, matching the notches in E and C, and insert a zipper in the middle of the C-B seam. Turn the cushion covers right side out through the zipper

opening. Fill the cover generously with foam chips and zipper up.

Slipstitch one strip of Velcro to the top of the chair back and another along the corresponding stretch of the A-B seam. Now press the cushion into position as shown in the photograph on page 49 and mold it into the back and over the arms of the chair.

To make the sofa you simply double the width of the back and front panels, the seat frame and the two blocks of foam. Support the seat frame with extra angle brackets. When it comes to making the cushion, add the extra width to the 'Fold' ends of pattern pieces A, B, C and D. If it is not possible to cut each of these extended pieces as one piece, make sure the joins in at least A and D occur in the corner angles of the cushion. Piece B, which of course widens towards the 'Fold', should be extended by a straight rectangular piece of the required length. The zipper and the Velcro strip holding the cushion in place will also need to be longer.

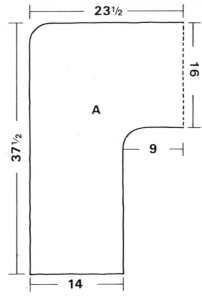

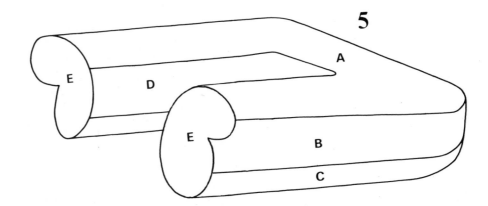

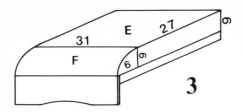

3

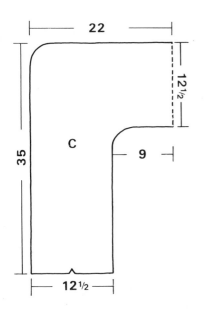

22

12½

35

C

9

12½

7

D

31

12

E

6

6

12¼

6¼

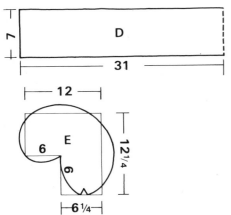

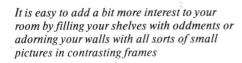

It is easy to add a bit more interest to your room by filling your shelves with oddments or adorning your walls with all sorts of small pictures in contrasting frames

BOLSTER SUITE

Chubby, roly-poly cushion furniture–just the thing to loll about in. These chairs and sofas are not expensive to make, though the choice of materials is yours, as always. So is the exclusive, untraditional comfort they provide.

Bold stripes emphasize the chunkiness of the Bolster Suite. Or you can make it up in red towelling, as we did, or in any other plain pile or bouclé fabric, for extra warmth and huggability. Made up in strong canvas the suite can be used out of doors.

Removable covers are not essential, but they stretch the lifetime of the suite because you can take them off for cleaning.

Another great thing about the Bolster Suite is that it is self supporting, and needs no hardware, apart from short lengths of wire to secure the headrests, and zips for the covers.

These pieces are quite hefty, so try a chair first and then build up the suite at your leisure.

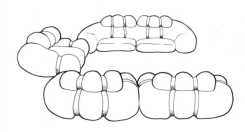

Materials needed for one chair
Inner cover fabric:
   9m–90cm wide (10yd–36in) or
   5.50m–120cm wide (6yd–48in)
Outer cover fabric: same as for inner
   cover
Zippers–for inner cover:
   one 50cm (20in) and two 40cm
     (16in)
Zippers–for outer cover:
   two 60cm (24in), one 45cm (18in),
     one 50cm (20in) and one 40cm
     (16in)
Foam rubber block: 53 × 43 × 10cm
   (21 × 17 × 4in)
Foam rubber chips
Webbing: 7m–6cm wide (8yd–2in wide)
Twine to secure webbing
Soft wire: 2.50m–4mm thick (3yd–⅛in
   thick)

Making a chair

Six separate pieces of fabric are needed for the U-shaped cylinder which makes the chair back and sides: two A pieces, one B, one C and two D's (see **Fig 1**). The foam rubber block which forms the base of the seat has a piece of fabric wrapped all the way around it and two end pieces, so you will need one F piece and two G's. Piece H is the cylindrical headrest and has an E piece at either end. All the measurements in **Fig 1** include 1cm (½in) seam allowances. **Fig 2** shows how all the pieces are assembled.

All the inner covers have zippers to make it easier to add to or plump up the stuffing from time to time. The 50cm (20in) zipper is inserted in the bottom back seam (between piece A and C) of the U cushion. The head rest has a 40cm (16in) zipper and so does the seat.

Stuff the U piece as tightly as possible but make the headrest a little softer. Pack the upper side of the seat block with foam chips as well.

Longer zippers are needed in the outer covers to make fitting and removal easier. Insert the two 60cm (24in) zippers in the bottom back seam of the U piece so that they meet in the middle of the closure. The 45cm (18in) zipper goes in the head rest.

Before making up the outer seat cover attach four loops of fabric to the underside of the cover as shown in **Fig 3**. These are designed to take the bands of webbing which hold the chair together and should be positioned about 10cm (4in) from the front and back edges of the seat. Now insert the 50 and 40cm (20 and 16in) zippers in the cover to allow as wide an opening as possible (i.e. both zippers meet in the same corner).

Fig 3 shows how the webbing is attached to the underside of the seat. You'll need three lengths of webbing, one 290cm (114in) long and two 160cm (64in) long. Make a firmly stitched loop at both ends of each length. Now run the longest length through the front loops on the seat bottom, up and over the chair sides, back under the seat again and through the loops again (**Fig 4**). Tie the ends of the webbing together with strong string or tape. The headrest, attached by two bands of webbing, is held in place by a rectangle of soft wire 6.5 × 20cm (2¼ × 8in) (**Fig 5**).

To make the sofa

The broken line which divides pattern piece A in half is the correct place to insert a sofa extension. If you insert an extra length of, say, 90cm (36in)–this would make the seat 133cm (53in) wide–pattern pieces B, C and G will also have to be extended by 90cm (36in). Piece F would need to be extended by twice 90cm (36in) because it has to go around the upper and lower side of the seat. You will also need two headrests (piece H) instead of one, and four headrest ends (piece E).

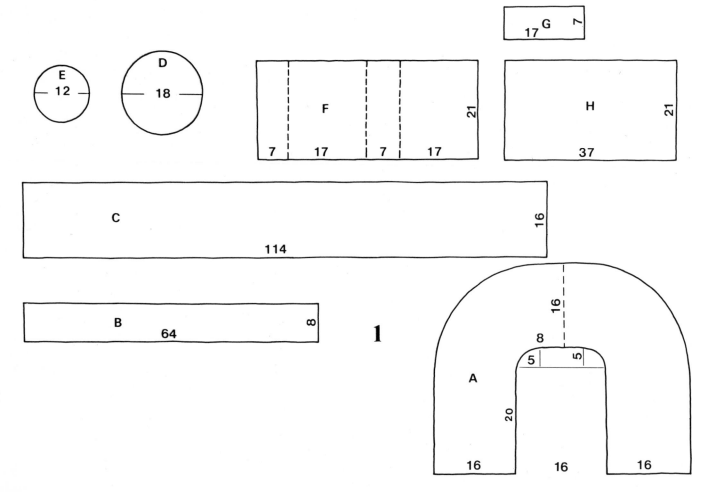

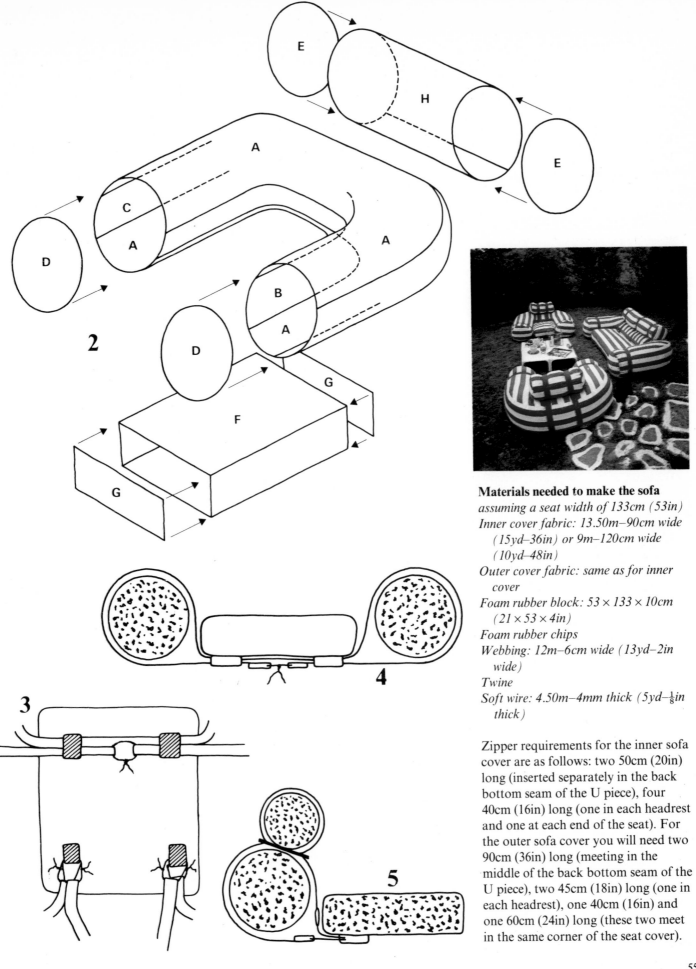

2

3

4

5

Materials needed to make the sofa

assuming a seat width of 133cm (53in)
Inner cover fabric: 13.50m–90cm wide
(15yd–36in) or 9m–120cm wide
(10yd–48in)
Outer cover fabric: same as for inner
cover
Foam rubber block: 53 × 133 × 10cm
(21 × 53 × 4in)
Foam rubber chips
Webbing: 12m–6cm wide (13yd–2in
wide)
Twine
Soft wire: 4.50m–4mm thick (5yd–$\frac{1}{8}$in
thick)

Zipper requirements for the inner sofa
cover are as follows: two 50cm (20in)
long (inserted separately in the back
bottom seam of the U piece), four
40cm (16in) long (one in each headrest
and one at each end of the seat). For
the outer sofa cover you will need two
90cm (36in) long (meeting in the
middle of the back bottom seam of the
U piece), two 45cm (18in) long (one in
each headrest), one 40cm (16in) and
one 60cm (24in) long (these two meet
in the same corner of the seat cover).

NEW TABLES

Here are six gloriously simple and elegant table ideas which neatly sidestep the problem of attaching legs to tops.

Blockboard makes the cheapest and most serviceable type of table top and ready-made wooden trestles (the sort sold for making wallpapering tables) make the simplest kind of legs. But you can also use chipboard or even an existing table. You'll find a board or glass top is quite heavy enough to rest on trestles without budging. We used glass–ask your glazier to cut it to the exact size–as well as board for some of the tables.

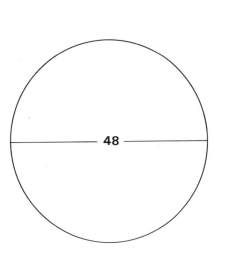

BREAKFAST TABLE

For this you will need a circular piece of blockboard 120cm (48in) in diameter and two blockboard base pieces 91.5 × 70cm (36 × 28in) (**Fig 1**). Your board should be at least 16mm ($\frac{5}{8}$in) thick. Cut a slot 35cm (14in) long by the thickness of the blockboard in the exact centre of each base piece and then saw out the four circles (these should be 35cm (14in) in diameter). Press filler into all the visible sawn edges, allow it to harden, then sand them down. Sand all the other visible surfaces as well. Apply two coats of primer and finish with polyurethane gloss paint. Slot the base pieces together.

The red 'place mats' are actually painted. We used a cardboard stencil to do this and gave the four areas two coats of polyurethane varnish.

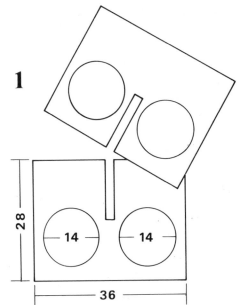

1

CLOTH TOP TABLE

This is a method of transferring to a table top the sensational patterns one often sees in curtain fabrics. The best fabric for the purpose is a medium-weight cotton with a tight weave. It is possible to achieve a gleaming, heat-resistant surface with successive coats of clear polyurethane varnish.

We replaced the top of an existing table with a piece of 2cm ($\frac{7}{8}$in) thick blockboard which we painted white (after edge filling, sanding and priming, naturally). White gives maximum luminosity to the color of any fabric you put on top. We then spread a synthetic resin adhesive (the sort you

mix with water) over the painted blockboard and smoothed the fabric over it. Your fabric should be thoroughly damp, not wringing wet, for this operation. A wooden ruler is very good for smoothing it flat and pressing out air bubbles.

Let the fabric dry thoroughly before you start varnishing. Apply three or four coats of varnish to start with, then sand carefully with a sanding block and wet sandpaper (i.e. 'wet and dry' silicon-carbide paper, widely used for sanding down paint or woodwork). Wipe off the sludgy residue with a damp cloth. Apply a final coat of varnish, then polish with a good brand

of wax/silicone polish.

Aluminum strip makes an elegant edge finish. Screwing it in place is generally more satisfactory than sticking it.

INVISIBLE TABLE

Sand, prime and paint two trestles, buy
a sheet of glass 130×75cm (52×30in)
and approximately 8mm ($\frac{3}{8}$in) thick
(ask the glazier to bevel the edges), and
that's all there is to it, apart from
putting the glass on the legs!

THREE GLASS TOP TABLES

All sorts of decorative items–posters, postcards, stamps, fabrics–can be sandwiched between a table top and a sheet of glass. We chose a length of wax shelf-lining paper, a romantic photo blow-up, and a selection of colour photographs from glossy magazines. The procedure in each case was the same.

First sand, prime and paint your trestles. Second, cut a piece of 12mm ($\frac{1}{2}$in) thick blockboard measuring 140×75cm (56×30in), then sand, prime and paint it. Third, place your photographs, paper, etc. on the top. Fourth, buy a piece of 4mm ($\frac{1}{6}$in) thick glass exactly the same size as the top and place it on top of the photographs, etc. Fifth, stick plastic edging strip (the flexible sort which has a lip at top and bottom–you'll need about 4.5m–5yd) all the way around the edges; it might be a good idea to tack the strip down with drawing pins at intervals until the adhesive dries.

In the case of the table with the white and green waxed paper top, we pasted a long strip of the same paper on the adjoining wall–a touch of chic which instantly makes the table part of the general decor.

Rescue a deckchair this weekend! If your deckchairs are beginning to look woebegone it won't take long to rejuvenate them. You can paint or stain and varnish the frame, and you can cushion or cover up faded or tattered canvas. Whatever beauty treatment you choose, it will brighten up your garden or patio no end.

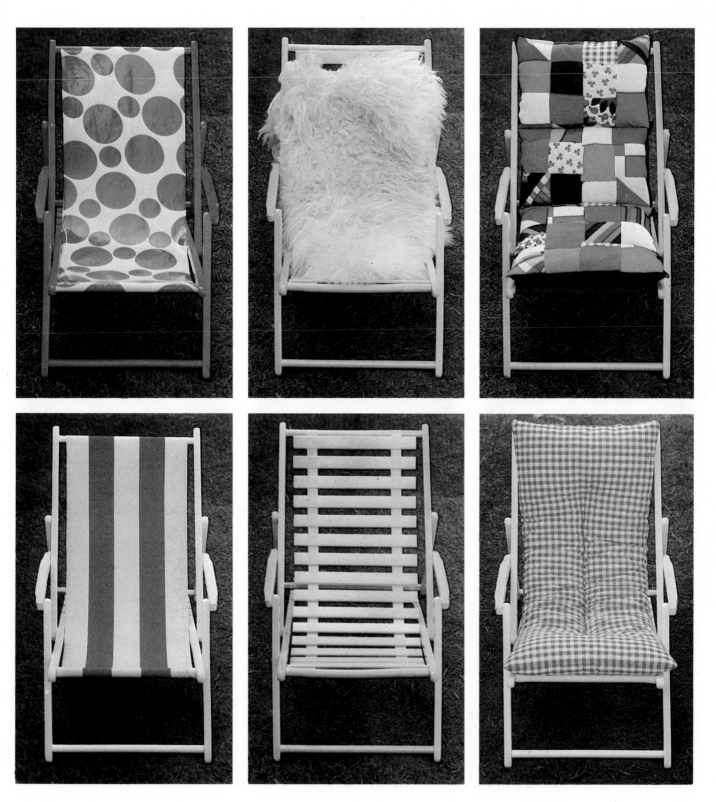

*From rags and tatters to redemption...
there are a hundred and one solutions to
beautifying old deckchairs, but we ran out
of washing line!*

General note

Use paint stripper and glasspaper or steel wool to remove old paint or varnish. Sand the wood and give it two coats of primer before painting it with polyurethane gloss paint. Or you can stain the wood–there are some gorgeous colours on the market today–and weatherproof it with clear polyurethane varnish.

If the canvas is simply stained or faded, a cover-up in a thinner prettier fabric is the most economical proposition–or you can give it the cushion treatment. Even if the canvas is torn, it might still be worth patching and then covering up or cushioning. In hopeless cases you will have to replace the canvas altogether.

Unless you buy special deckchair canvas, which comes in narrow widths, wide fabrics (140cm–54in–and over) are more economical for covering up or replacing old canvas than narrower ones. A standard deckchair, including allowances for finishing edges and tacking them to the frame, takes approx. 50 × 140cm (20 × 54in). But always measure the chair first, if you are replacing the canvas. **Fig 1** shows the two measurements you need to take with the chair in the reclining position. Add about 20cm (8in) for wrapping around the dowels at each end, and about 5cm (2in) on the width to allow for a hem down each side.

Operation cover-up

The quickest cover-up method–no laborious hand-stitching–is as follows. Remove the old canvas from the chair and lay it out flat on the wrong side of your cover-up fabric. Cut out a piece of fabric approx. 2.5cm (1in) wider all around than the canvas. Fold the edges over the canvas and pin a hem all round. Now machine stitch canvas and cover-up fabric together round all four edges, stitching about 1cm ($\frac{3}{8}$in) from the edge. Run an extra line of stitching along both short edges. Replace the rescued canvas on the chair and tack the ends to the underside of the dowels with flat-headed nails.

Cushion treatment

All sorts of cushions can be made to fit a standard deckchair, assuming the existing canvas is serviceable. These rest on the canvas and are kept in place with tape ties around the top dowel. For each cushion you will need two pieces of fabric approximately 60 × 150cm (24 × 60in). Make your lines of quilting stitching *before* you stuff the cushions and remember to leave openings to poke the stuffing through.

The patchwork cushion (A in **Fig 2**) has three rows of stitching which quilt it into four equal rectangles, plus a row of stitching around all edges, $\frac{1}{2}$cm ($\frac{1}{4}$in) from the edge, to finish them. The finished size of the cushion before stuffing should be approx. 12cm (5in) longer and 5cm (2in) wider than the canvas. When you stuff it it will plump out and still cover the canvas generously.

The white quilted cushion (B in **Fig 2**) is a variation on the same theme. Again the finished size of the cushion before stuffing should be longer and wider than the canvas. We made the two head panels approx. 40cm (16in) deep and the rest approx. 28cm (11in) square. All the edges have a line of stitching to finish and firm them.

The same general remarks about allowing room for stuffing and about edge stitching apply to the pink quilted cushion (C in **Fig 2**) and to the gingham cushion (D in **Fig 2**). The pink cushion however needs to be approx. 25cm (10in) longer than the canvas before stuffing because its front panel hangs over the edge of the seat. Here the top panel is approx. 35cm (14in) deep, the front panel 12cm (5in) deep

and the others 20cm (8in) deep. The gingham cushion has a single central line of stitching which stops approx. 30cm (12in) from either end of the cushion. The diagonal red and white stripe chair has a neck cushion only. This measures approx. 50 × 35cm (20 × 14in) and is cut so that it continues the line of the stripes.

In the case of A, B and C you could make the cushion washable by making mini inner cushions for each panel which you remove through zippered or oversewn closures.

Replacing the canvas

Stout fabrics are in order here–cottons, linens, heavy duty plastic–in bold stripes, floral prints or plain with appliqué motifs. Simply cut a piece of fabric approx. 5cm (2in) wider and approx. 20cm (8in) longer than your tape measurement (**Fig 1**) and hem it to the correct width. Make a narrow hem along both ends and attach them to the chair with upholstery tacks or flat-headed nails.

Another idea which works very well is a slatted back and seat (the yellow chair). You'll need about 15 or 16 pieces of 9mm ($\frac{3}{8}$in) thick wooden batten about 5cm (2in) wide and a shade shorter than the width of the chair, two lengths of webbing about 1.70m ($1\frac{3}{4}$yd) long and a few dozen flat-headed nails for attaching the webbing to the battens and to the chair. Sand, prime and paint the battens first of course.

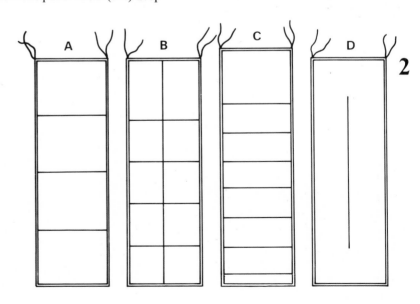

2

1

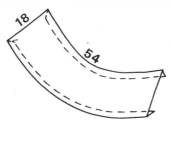

18

54

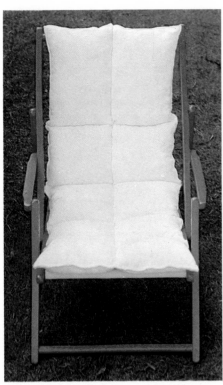

BEDS & BEDROOMS

SEW-UP SUPERBEDS

If you think spending a third of your life in bed is too much, have another think! A Sew-up Superbed is much more than a bed–it's a bed, a settee, a chair and a card table all rolled into one deliciously soft and sensual piece of furniture rather like a luxury indoor liferaft!

The Superbed concept is simple: a floor mattress with a big fat tubular cushion all the way round it. There is also a backrest pillow which can be adapted to hold sheets and blankets during the day.

Making a Superbed is no more than a day's work (the big ring pillows are simply tubes joined at both ends). We put the Circular Superbed on a platform–a good idea if your floor is cold or if you want to raise the general level of the room–as the only piece of furniture in the room. As you can see from the photographs the Rectangular Superbed looks fine on the floor because the general level of the room coincides with the top of the wainscoting.

Hunt around old clothes shops for interesting pieces of velvet or velveteen for the ring pillows, or buy old velvet curtains at warehouse auctions, and make them up into sumptuous patchwork.

RECTANGULAR SUPERBED

Materials needed

Foam rubber block for mattress:
  *120 × 190 × 15 or 20cm (48 × 75 × 6
  or 8in)*
*Fabric: total amount needed is 20.50m
  –90cm wide (23yd–36in) or
  14.10m–120cm wide (15½yd–48in)*
*Ring pillow: 13.80m–90cm wide
  (15¼yd–36in) or 10.50m–120cm wide
  (11½yd–48in)*
*Backrest pillow: 2m–90cm wide
  (2¼yd–36in) or 1.60m–120cm wide
  (1¾yd–48in)*
*Mattress cover: 4.70m–90cm wide
  (5½yd–36in) or 3.50m–120cm wide
  (4yd–48in)*
*Webbing 8–10cm (3–4in) wide:
  approx. 4m (4½yd)*
Nylon string
*Zippers: two 40cm (16in) long for ring
  pillow, two 75cm (30in) long (or one
  40cm (16in) long) for backrest*
Foam rubber chips.

We have quoted separate fabric
requirements for the ring pillow,
backrest pillow and mattress cover in
case you want to make them in
different fabrics.

Fig 1 gives the dimensions of the
pattern pieces (A, B, C, D and E) for
the ring pillow. All dimensions include
a 1cm (½in) seam allowance. You will
need to cut eight A pieces, four B's,
four C's, one D and one E.

Sew the A, B and C pieces together
first to make the top and bottom of the
ring **(Fig 2)**, leaving one of the A–B
seams open in each case (see arrows).
Stitch E to the outer and D to the inner
edges of the top and bottom ring to
form a long tube open at both ends.
Remember to leave two 40cm (16in)
openings in the seam joining the two B
pieces of the bottom ring to D. Turn
right sides out and insert the two
zippers. Leave one zipper open. Turn
the tube inside out through the open
zipper and stitch the open ends of the
tube together, right sides together, as
far as you can go. Turn the tube right
side out again through the zipper and
finish seaming the ends of the tube
together. You now have a closed
rectangular ring ready to be filled with
foam rubber chips. Whether you pack

the foam tightly or loosely depends on
the degree of resilience you require.

The mattress cover, pattern pieces H
and I in **Fig 3**, is made by hemming one
long edge of I, threading the hem with
nylon string, stitching the other long
edge to H all the way around and
stitching the two ends of I together.
Measurements given include 1cm (½in)
seam allowances. Smooth the cover
over the mattress, turn the mattress
upside down, pull the drawstring tight,
and tie the ends.

The backrest pillow is a cylinder

with a circle at either end (F and G in
Fig 3). If you want to use it as a
daytime hide-away for bedclothes
include two 75cm (30in) zippers in the
160cm (63in) seam which makes F into
a cylinder. The zippers should meet in
the middle of the seam. If you intend to
stuff the pillow with foam chips then a
40cm (16in) zip will do. **Figs 6–8** and
text on page 77 explain how the
backrest pillow is attachable to the ring
pillow. Your three bands of webbing
would need to be approx. 130cm (52in)
long.

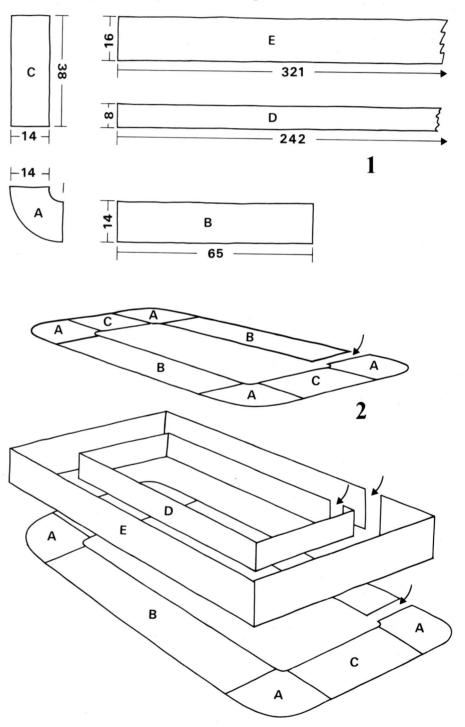

Circular Superbed – *instructions overleaf*

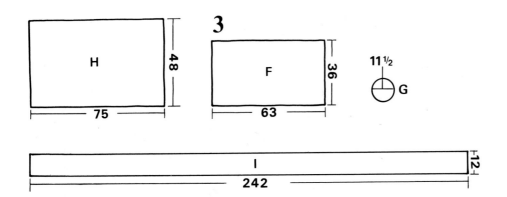

H — 75 × 48

3 F — 63 × 36

11½ G

I — 242 × 12

CIRCULAR SUPERBED

Materials needed

*Foam rubber for mattress: circular
 block 2m (80in) diameter × 15cm
 (6in) thick or two semicircular blocks
 stuck together*
*Fabric: total amount needed is 19.50m
 –90cm wide (21½yd–36in) or
 15.10m–120cm wide (16½yd–48in)*
*Mattress cover (A and B in Fig 4):
 8.30m–90cm wide (9¼yd–36in) or
 5.80m–120cm wide (6½yd–48in)*
*Ring pillow (C in Fig 4): 8.20m–90 or
 120cm wide (9yd–36 or 48in)*
*Backrest pillow (D and E in Fig 4):
 3m–90cm wide (3¼yd–36in) or
 2.70m–120cm wide (3yd–48in)*
Zippers: three 40cm (16in) long
*Webbing 8–10cm (3–4in) wide to
 secure backrest: approx. 10m (11yd)*
Nylon string
*Wire 3mm (⅛in) diameter: approx.
 2.20m (2½yd)*
10 D-rings same width as webbing
Foam rubber chips

Fig 4 shows the dimensions of all the
fabric pieces required (1cm (½in) seam
allowances are included) and **Fig 5**
shows where each piece occurs in the
finished article.

The circular part of the mattress
cover (A in **Fig 4**) should be cut from a
rectangle of fabric made from three
90cm (36in) or two 120cm (48in)
widths of fabric stitched together. Lay
the fabric flat on the floor to draw the
circle. Pin the exact centre point of the
rectangle to the floor with a panel pin,
tie a length of string around the pin,
mark the length of radius
required–100cm (40in)–and use chalk
to draw the circle. As B is not visible in
the finished article it can be made up
by joining several pieces of fabric
together.

Before you stitch A to B make a hem
along one side of B and thread it with
nylon string. This draws tight under
the mattress to keep the cover in place
and is tied with a bow.

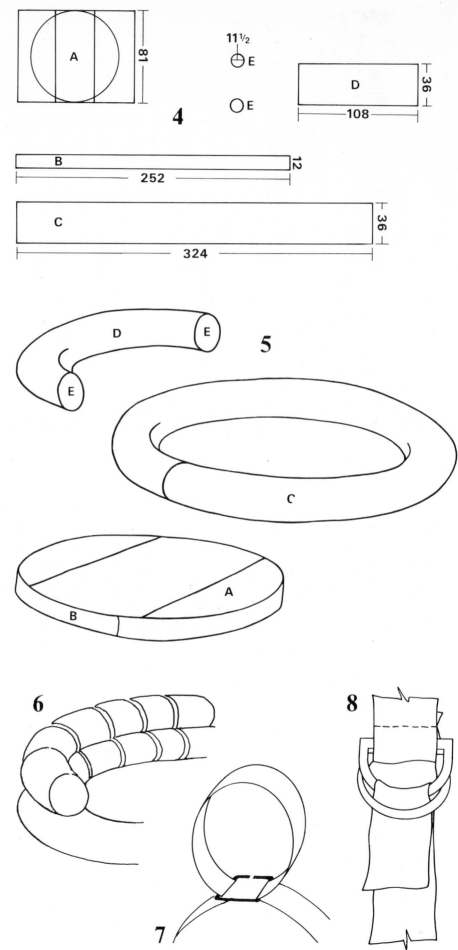

The ring pillow is just a tube with its ends joined. Make the tube by stitching the long edges of C together, leaving two 40cm (16in) gaps for the two zippers. Insert both zippers and leave them open. Pull both ends of the tube through one of the open zippers and stitch them together–right sides together of course–as far as you can go. Then pull the unseamed ends back through one of the zippers and finish the seam. You now have a continuous circular tube like a huge doughnut!

The backrest pillow is made by stitching the long edges of D together to form a tube, leaving a 40cm (16in) opening for the zipper. Insert the zipper and leave it open. Turn the tube inside out. Baste and stitch the circular E pieces to the ends, then turn right side out through the open zipper.

Fill the ring and backrest pillow with foam chips. The tighter the filling the better they look.

The backrest pillow is kept in place by bands of webbing **(Fig 6)** which thread through pieces of wire bent into rectangles approximately 10cm (4in) long by the width of the webbing **(Fig 6)**. **Fig 8** shows how the bands of webbing, five in all, are kept tight by means of D-rings.

77

A four-poster bed is a popular pipe dream but old four-posters are very difficult to track down and very expensive to buy. So why not make your own? Like a lot of things it's simple when you know how.

The problem with old four-posters is that they were built for lofty rooms, not for modern apartments, and judging by their length and narrowness, for short and solitary occupants! But the four-poster concept makes just as much sense in this supersonic age as it did a hundred years ago. If you are trying to cut down on heating bills why not take your books, television set, telephone, typewriter, card games and cups of tea into the bedroom and keep warm under the blankets? After all the vast majority of us need to feel snug and cosy. A four-poster with the curtains drawn becomes a den for one, for two or for the whole family, a small comfortable world where you can play, eat, work . . . and sleep.

These are the thoughts we had in mind when we designed this modern double-bed-size four-poster. It is made mostly of chipboard and can be dismantled in ten minutes. Delegate the various jobs involved–have one person make the drapes, someone else do the sanding and painting, and so on.

Materials needed

Chipboard 19mm ($\frac{3}{4}$in) thick:
  1 piece 176 × 80cm (68 × 32in) for bedhead (A)
  1 piece 176 × 67cm (68 × 26$\frac{1}{2}$in) for foot of bed (B)
  2 pieces 196 × 40cm (78 × 16in) for sides (C)
  2 pieces 196 × 15cm (78 × 6in) for canopy (D)
  2 pieces 176 × 15cm (68 × 6in) for canopy (E)

Wood:
  4 poles 214cm (85in) long × 5.7cm (2$\frac{1}{4}$in) diameter for bedposts (F)
  1 piece 200 × 3.5 × 5.8cm (80 × 1$\frac{1}{2}$ × 2$\frac{1}{4}$in) for centre strut (G)
  2 pieces 1.3cm ($\frac{1}{2}$in) dowel 175cm (67$\frac{1}{2}$in) long for awning (H)
  3.5 × 3.5cm (1$\frac{1}{2}$ × 1$\frac{1}{2}$in) section for frame of mattress base:
    2 pieces 196cm (78in) long (see C in Fig 2)
    4 pieces 86$\frac{1}{4}$cm (33$\frac{1}{4}$in) long (see A and B in Fig 2)
    2 pieces 10cm (4in) long (see A and B in Fig 2)
  batten 5.6cm (2$\frac{1}{4}$in) wide × 9mm ($\frac{3}{8}$in) thick: 18 pieces 180cm (70in) long for slatted mattress base

Foam rubber block for mattress:
  200 × 180 × 15cm (80 × 70 × 6in)
50 chipboard screws 5cm (2in) long
*32 knock-down fixings (or 4m of 1cm (13$\frac{1}{2}$ft of $\frac{3}{8}$in) wooden dowel, 32 chipboard screws 16mm ($\frac{5}{8}$in) long and 32 wood screws 5cm (2in) long) for attaching bedposts
6 cup hooks for holding awning rods
Lightweight curtain track, with gliders:
  2 pieces 196cm (78in) long, 2 pieces 176cm (68in) long
Filler, file, sandpaper, primer, paint
Webbing 4cm (1$\frac{1}{2}$in) wide: 4m (4$\frac{1}{2}$yd)
Sheeting for awning: 1 piece 208 × 182cm (83 × 71in)
Fabric for drapes: 31m–90cm wide (34yd–36in) or 24.50m–120cm wide (27yd–48in)–for full drapes but less if you are happy with a less opulent look
Rufflette tape or curtain heading, with hooks: 16.50m (18$\frac{1}{4}$yd)

*These knock-down fixings have four compatible components: a steel thread 12cm long × 6mm (5 × $\frac{1}{4}$in) diameter; a retaining nut with a hole 6mm ($\frac{1}{4}$in) diameter through which the thread screws; a round-headed capping nut, with a washer, which screws onto the other end of the thread. See diagram.

There are two ways of cutting the curvaceous A, B and C pieces in **Fig 1** –doing it yourself or persuading your lumber dealer to do it! In either case make a full size cardboard template of each piece (**Fig 1** shows exactly half of each piece). You need one A, one B and two C's in 19mm ($\frac{3}{4}$in) chipboard.

Fig 2 shows the measurements of the other chipboard and wood components. Cut two D and two E pieces (in chipboard) for the canopy, four F's (in 5.7cm ($2\frac{1}{4}$in) dowel) for the bedposts, one G (wood) for the centre strut which supports the slatted mattress base, and two H's (in 1.3cm ($\frac{1}{2}$in) dowel) for suspending the awning.

Fig 3 overleaf shows where pieces A–H go in the finished bed. Finished inside dimensions are 200×180cm (80×70in), the same size as the mattress.

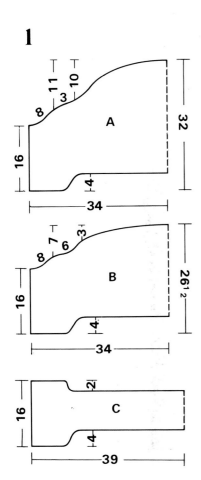

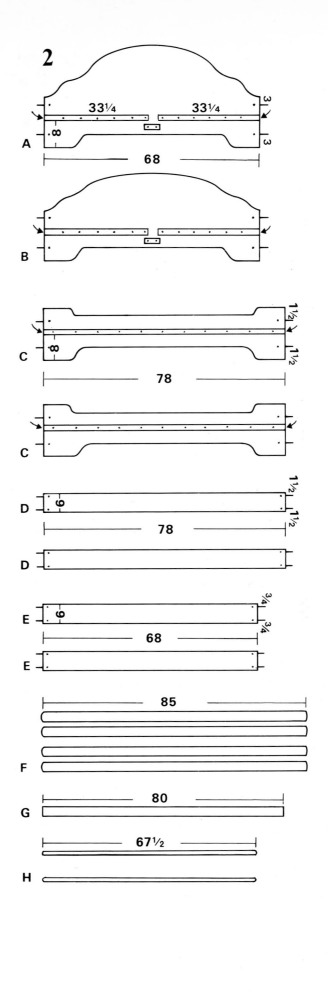

3

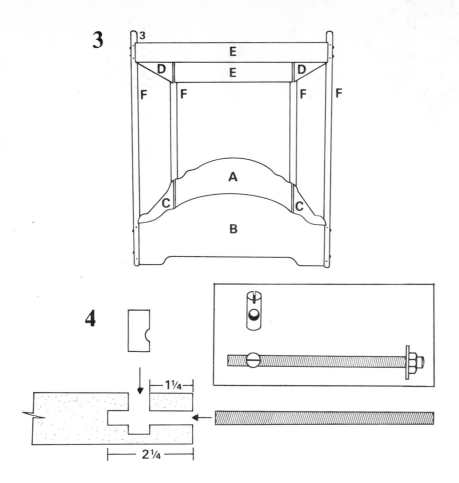

4

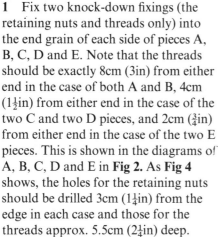

1 Fix two knock-down fixings (the retaining nuts and threads only) into the end grain of each side of pieces A, B, C, D and E. Note that the threads should be exactly 8cm (3in) from either end in the case of both A and B, 4cm (1½in) from either end in the case of the two C and two D pieces, and 2cm (¾in) from either end in the case of the two E pieces. This is shown in the diagrams of A, B, C, D and E in **Fig 2**. As **Fig 4** shows, the holes for the retaining nuts should be drilled 3cm (1¼in) from the edge in each case and those for the threads approx. 5.5cm (2¼in) deep.

If knock-down fixings are not available then 1cm (⅜in) wooden dowel pegs 12cm (5in) long will serve. Drill holes 1cm (⅜in) diameter into the end grain of pieces A, B, C, D and E as outlined above, insert the dowel pegs and screw them in place with 16mm (⅝in) chipboard screws.

2 Assuming you are using knock-down fixings, drill holes 6mm (¼in) in diameter all the way through the diameter of the bedposts at heights corresponding with the heights of the

threads just inserted into A, B, C, D and E. Note that the bottom edges of A, B and C rest on the floor but that the top edges of D and E are 8cm (3in) from the top of the posts **(Fig 3)**. If you are using dowel fixings the holes in the bedposts need to be 1cm (⅜in) diam.

3 A, B and C in **Fig 2** show the exact positions of the 3.5cm (1¼in) square-section pieces of wood which make the frame on which the slatted mattress base rests. Saw off their adjoining corners (see arrows in **Fig 2** and black and white photographs) at an angle of 45° before screwing them to their respective pieces of chipboard. The two 10cm (4in) lengths of wood should then be screwed below the gaps in the wood just screwed to A and B. Make sure their top edge is exactly 5.8cm (2¼in) below the top of the gap. The ends of the strut (G) slot into these gaps.

4 Now you can start assembling the bed, as shown in the photographs. Screw a washer and capping nut onto the end of each protruding thread (or saw off the ends of the dowel pegs

flush with the posts, and screw them in place through the diameter of the posts using 5cm (2in) wood screws).

5 The slats which make the mattress base are tacked or stapled to a 2m (80in) length of webbing at each side–distance between the slats should be 6cm (2⅜in). The slats rest on the wooden frame fixed to the inside of A, B and C and on the centre strut G.

6 Screw three cup hooks (one at each end and one in the middle) close to the top inside edges of each E piece to hold the awning dowels.

7 Fill all visible chipboard edges as shown in the photograph. When the filler has set hard, sand and prime all wood and chipboard surfaces. Give them another rub down with fine glasspaper and paint in the color of your choice. Use a roller to paint the large areas–it saves time.

8 Screw the lengths of curtain tracking, with their gliders, to the undersides of the canopy.

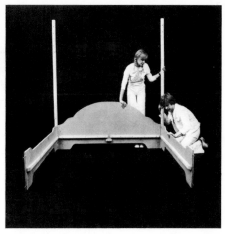

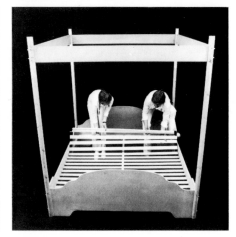

9 Make a very narrow hem down both long sides of your piece of sheeting. The short sides should have a 5cm (2in) hem to take the 1.3cm ($\frac{1}{2}$in) dowels. When in position the awning should be taut, kept in place by the cup hooks holding the dowels at either end.

10 The length of curtain fabric quoted allows a drop of 175cm (70in) for the side drapes and a drop of 170cm (68in) for the back and front drapes (both dimensions include an allowance for top and bottom hems). It also allows for an ungathered width of 225 or 240cm (90 or 96in), i.e. two and a half 90cm (36in) widths or two 120cm (48in) widths on each of the four side drapes and an ungathered width of 180cm (72in), i.e. two 90cm (36in) widths or one and a half 120cm (48in) widths, on each of the back and front drapes.

Cotton gingham was our choice for the drapes because it is gay, machine-washable and inexpensive.

Just a detail from the room – but details make rooms

83

VIKING DOUBLE BED

Take a platform, add a backrest, put a mattress in the middle, and you have a bed. Make the platform wider, shape the backrest, finish with stained pinewood and shiny steel bolts, and you have a bed which is very elegant, very strong and completely personal.

Have a look at the prices of double beds with even a soupçon of new thinking in their design and we guarantee you'll be at your local lumber yard within a week!

The picture-frame surround to the Viking Double Bed does duty as a bedside table. We used pine wall cladding for this as well as for the bedhead.

A splash of colour for a dark corner of the room

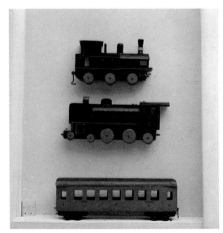

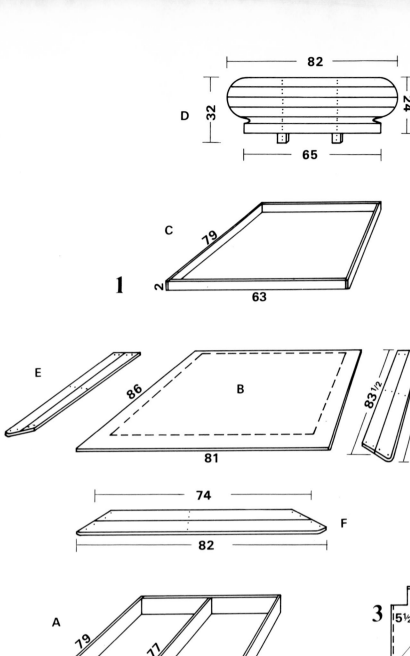

D 82 24 32 65

C 79 2 63

1

E 86 81 **B** 83½ 87½ **E**

74 **F** 82

A 79 77 6 63

10½ **2** 11 8½ 27 8

3 5½ 5½ 89 12 75

Materials needed

Base (A)
  Wood 15 cm (6in) wide × 2cm (1in)
    thick:
    2 pieces 200cm (79in) long
    2 pieces 160cm (63in) long
    1 piece 196cm (77in) long
Baseboard (B)
  Chipboard 16mm (⅝in) thick:
    1 piece 217 × 204mm (86 × 81in)
    or 2 pieces 217 × 102cm (86 × 40½in)
Mattress frame (C)
  Wood 5cm (2in) wide × 2cm (1in):
    2 pieces 199cm (79in) long
    2 pieces 160cm (63in) long
Headboard (D)
  Cladding 10cm (4in) wide × 2cm(⅞in)
    thick:
    5 pieces 207cm (82in) long
    1 piece 164cm (65in) long
    2 pieces 81cm long (32in)
Side surround (E) foot surround (F):
  Cladding 10cm (4in) wide × 2cm (⅞in)
    thick:
    2 pieces 210cm (83½in) long (E)
    2 pieces 219cm (87½in) long (E)
    1 piece 185cm (74in) long (F)
    1 piece 207cm (82in) long (F)
Round headed bolts 5cm (2½in): 64
3.5cm (1½in) angle brackets: 4
Wood screws, chipboard screws
Rasp, glasspaper
Woodstain, polyurethane varnish
Foam rubber block for mattress
    195 × 169 × 15cm (77 × 63 × 6in)

Screw together the five pieces of wood which make the base (A in **Fig 1**). The baseboard (B in **Fig 1**) is then screwed to the base. Use chipboard screws for this. The head end of the base and the baseboard should be flush, the one exactly centered on the other as indicated by the broken lines. (To provide ventilation beneath the foam rubber mattress it is advisable to drill holes of about 1cm (⅜in) diameter at intervals of 30cm (12in) in the baseboard.)

The next step is to screw together the four pieces of wood which make the mattress frame (C in **Fig 1**). Center the frame on the base board, one end flush with its head end, and screw it in place with four 3.5cm (1½in) angle brackets, one in the middle of each side.

To make the headboard (D in **Fig 1**) align the five 207cm (82in) lengths of cladding side by side on the floor and

center the 164cm (65in) length along the side of the last one. The two 81cm (32in) lengths, the vertical supports of the headboard, have to be bolted to them (**Fig 2**). So drill a row of bolt holes, two to each width of cladding, down either side of the headboard 70cm (27in) from each side. Then drill a corresponding row of holes down each support. Now bolt the headboard and supports together. Mark identical curves at either end of the headboard following the dimensions given in **Fig 2,** and saw off the excess with a coping saw. Use a pair of bolts to attach the bottom of each support to the wooden base of the bed.

The cladding panels which make the foot and side surrounds of the bed (F and E in **Fig 1**) have to have their corners sawn off at an angle of 45° where they butt together. Bolt the panels nearest the mattress frame to the baseboard, leaving a 1cm (⅜in) gap between them and the mattress frame. Finally round off all the cut and rough edges and sand them smooth. Stain all visible surfaces and finish with clear varnish.

Making the mattress cover
Fits mattress 195 × 160 × 15cm (77 × 63 × 6in)

The red and white teddy-bear-look cover shown here takes 2.70m (3yd) of 120cm (48in)-wide white fabric and the same of red. **Fig 3** shows the finished dimensions of the cover before the corners are sewn together.

To make it up cut the red and white fabric into long strips 32cm (13in) wide (this allows for 1cm (½in) seams). Stitch the strips together, alternating red and white, to make a rectangle 194 × 229cm (77 × 91in). Cut the first strip as a right angled triangle of side 32cm (13in). Lay it flat on the floor. Place the next strip beside the hypotenuse (the diagonal side) and cut it as if you were continuing the other two sides of the triangle, and so on. We used five white strips and four red.

Next hem all the edges of the rectangle so that it measures 190 × 225cm (75 × 89in). Now cut away a 14cm (5½in) square from each corner, sew up the corners (allowing 1cm (½in) on the seams) and fit over the mattress.

QUILTED BEDSPREADS

1

If you're wanting to brighten up a bedroom, an eye-catching quilt with matching cushions or rug is a simple answer. We used only simple quilting techniques for our quilts–just straightforward machine-quilted lines.

You may not be able to match the fabrics we used, but no matter. Just choose something similar that compliments your existing color scheme, or use the basic idea and interpret it in your own way.

If you are new to quilting, then the Reversible Squares Quilt or its matching mat is a good way in. The quilting on both these items is done on manageable size squares.

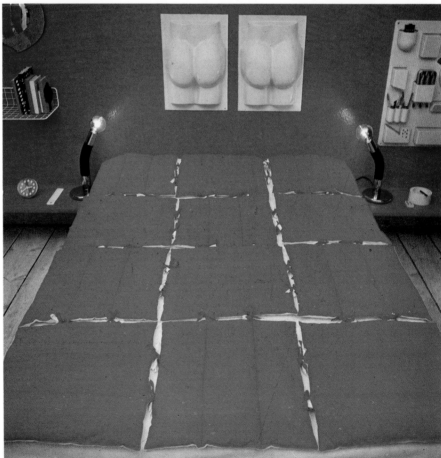

Materials needed

White fabric: 12 pieces 52 × 52cm
  (20½ × 20½in)
Red fabric: 12 pieces 52 × 52cm
  (20½ × 20½in)
Thick cotton wadding: 12 pieces
  50 × 50cm (19½ × 19½in)
68 white tapes, 68 red, 20cm (8in) long

REVERSIBLE SQUARES QUILT

Finished size approx. 160 × 200cm (5½ × 7ft). Suitable for 160cm (5½ft) double bed.

The quilt consists of 12 quilted squares tied together by tapes. Each square has a white and a red side and two lines of quilting. So by swapping the squares around you can create a bold checker pattern or keep the quilt plain on both sides. In either case, the quilting lines make their own pattern (see **Fig 1**). You will want 6 squares with tapes on 3 sides, 4 with tapes on 2 sides, and 2 with tapes on 4 sides.

To make up one square work as follows. Take one white and one red piece of fabric, and with the right sides facing, pin together around the edges, leaving most of one side open to take the wadding.

Take four tape lengths for each appropriate side and pin the two pairs of tapes in the seam–a white and a red tape in each pair. Remember that the long ends of the tapes should lie between the two layers of fabric (**Fig 2**). Position the pairs of tapes 18cm (7in) in from the corners of the square. Now stitch the layers together (allowing a 1cm (½in) seam) catching the tapes in the seam.

Turn the cover right side out and insert the wadding, pushing it well into the corners. Stitch closed the open side turning in the 1cm (½in) seam allowance and including two more pairs of tapes in the seam if necessary. To give the square a firm neat edge, run a line of stitching 2cm (¾in) in from the edge on all sides. Make up the other squares in the same way. Lay all the squares on the floor as if ready to tie them together with the same color uppermost. Take each square in turn and machine stitch the two lines of quilting (**Fig 3**) referring carefully to **Fig 1** to check their direction in relation to the tape ties. Finally tie all the squares together in the pattern you prefer.

Matching Mat

Finished size approx. 100cm (40in) square

Materials needed

White fabric: 16 pieces 27 × 27cm (11 × 11in)
Red fabric: 16 pieces 27 × 27cm (11 × 11in)
Cotton wadding: 16 pieces 25 × 25cm (10 × 10in)
24 white, 24 red tapes, 20cm (8in) long

Make up the squares as for the bedspread but omit the quilting and use just one pair of tapes on each side (**Fig 4**). You will need 4 squares with tapes on 4 sides, 8 squares with tapes on 3 sides, and 4 with tapes on 2 sides. Arrange these in a four by four square.

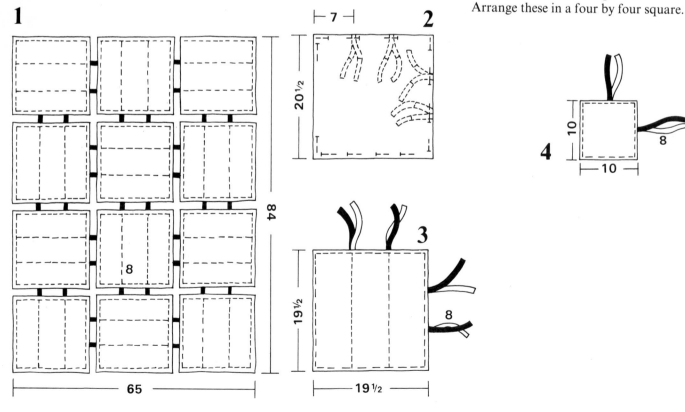

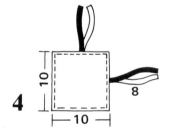

PATTERNED BEDSPREAD WITH BORDER
Finished size approx. 160 × 200cm
(5½ × 7ft). Suitable for 160cm (5½ft)
double bed.

Materials needed
Plain fabric: 2 pieces 202 × 162cm
    (84 × 67in) (includes 1cm (½in) seam
    allowance)
Patterned fabric: 1 piece 173 × 134cm
    (73½ × 57in) (includes 2 cm (1in) hem
    allowance)
Thick cotton wadding: 1 piece
    200 × 160cm (83 × 66in)

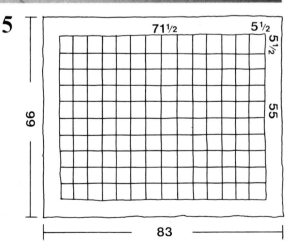

5

First iron under a 2cm (1in) hem along all sides of the patterned fabric. Lay this panel right side up on the right side of a plain piece. Make sure that the patterned panel is centered, then pin and slipstitch (or machine stitch) it to the plain fabric.

With right sides facing, pin and tack the other plain piece to the outer edge of the plain border. Machine stitch the two plain layers together round the edges, allowing a 1cm ($\frac{1}{2}$in) seam, leaving most of one side open to take the wadding. Turn the cover right side out.

Insert the layer of wadding, taking care to push it well into the corners and making sure it lies flat. Then pin and tack through all layers around the edge of the patterned panel. Stitch closed the opening.

The central panel is quilted by stitching small crosses at regular intervals. To position these crosses, first mark a grid of 13cm (5$\frac{1}{2}$in) squares (**Fig 5**), using tailors' chalk. At each line intersection pin, tack and machine stitch a cross about 4cm (1$\frac{1}{2}$in) long through all layers, using zig-zag stitch (**Fig 6**).

To emphasize and finish the border, simply run a line of stitching around the edge of the patterned panel. Make sure you have removed all the pins!

Matching Cushion
Finished size 64cm (25in) square

Materials needed for 1 cushion
Plain fabric: 2 pieces 66 × 66cm
(26 × 26in) which includes 1cm ($\frac{1}{2}$in)
seam allowances
Patterned fabric: 1 piece 48 × 48cm
(19 × 19in) which includes 2cm (1in)
seam allowances
Foam chips for filling

Make up the cushion in the same way as the bedspread, allowing a 10cm (4in) border, and fill with foam chips.

Small Blanket
Finished size approx. 44 × 120cm (18 × 50in)

Materials needed
Plain fabric: 2 pieces 122.5 × 46cm
(50$\frac{1}{2}$ × 19in) (includes 1cm–$\frac{1}{2}$in–seam
allowance)
Patterned fabric: 1 piece 114.5 × 38cm
(47$\frac{1}{2}$ × 16in) (includes 2cm–1in–hem
allowance)
Thick cotton wadding: 1 piece
120 × 44cm (49$\frac{1}{2}$ × 18in)

Make up as for the bedspread, allowing a 5cm (2in) plain border, and quilt the crosses at 8.5cm (3$\frac{1}{2}$in) intervals. This piece of quilting could equally well be used as a deckchair cover, a bedside rug or even a cot quilt.

QUILTED SCARF BEDSPREAD
Finished size approx. 130 × 200cm (4$\frac{1}{2}$ × 7ft). Suitable for a 90 or 105cm (3 or 3$\frac{1}{2}$ft) single bed, depending on how much drop you want at the sides.

Materials needed
Plain fabric: 2 pieces 132 × 202cm
(52 × 80in) (includes 1cm ($\frac{1}{2}$in) seam
allowance)
Matching scarves: 6, approx. 50 × 50cm
(20 × 20in)
Thick cotton wadding: 1 piece
130 × 200cm (51 × 79in)

Make up the cover in exactly the same way as the Patterned Bedspread with Border, substituting six scarves for the patterned panel. Position the scarves as

6

5½   1½

5½

49½

2

3½   3½

18

2

14

45½

shown in **Fig 7,** so that you have an
even border of the plain background
material all round, and balanced
spacing between the scarves.

After inserting the wadding, quilt
round the edges of the scarves and
along the broken lines shown in **Fig 7**
to complete the border. Also quilt
along any suitable pattern lines within
the scarf squares.

Matching Cushion
Finished size approx. 60 × 55cm
(23 × 21in) plus lace edging

Materials needed for 1 cushion
*Plain fabric: 2 pieces 62 × 57cm
   (24 × 22in) (includes 1cm (½in) seam
   allowance)*

*1 scarf to compliment bedspread design
Cotton lace: 2.5m (8ft), dyed to match
   color in scarf
Foam rubber chips for filling*

Slipstitch or machine stitch the scarf to
the right side of a plain fabric piece.
Then pin and tack the lace around the
edge of the plain fabric on the right
side—the frill should lie in towards the
center of the fabric. Place the other
piece of plain fabric right side down on
the lace and sew the cover together,
allowing a 1cm (½in) seam, and leaving
an opening on one side for the filling.
Turn the cover right side out, fill with
the foam chips, then sew up the
opening keeping the lace edging firmly
sandwiched in the seam.

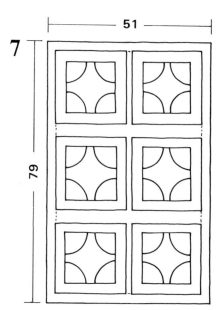

PATCHWORK COVERS

Beautiful patchworks are a traditional way of using up remnants but still one of the best. So we revived the technique to create some eyecatching bed covers. No need to stick to one kind of fabric, we used all sorts–cotton, velvet, corduroy, velour and terry cloth–picked up cheaply at sales. Large-scale patchwork patterns like ours look bright and stylish and don't take long to put together. But spend a little time making sure you get the maximum number of pieces out of your fabric. Bind the seams if you don't intend to line your cover.

STRIPED COVER
Finished size 264 × 250cm (105 × 100in)
(suitable for double bed)

Materials needed
*Ten fabrics: 90 × 80cm (36 × 32in) of
each*

For this cover we used all kinds of
different fabrics–velour, cottons, velvet
etc. Cut each piece of fabric into three
strips along its length. Sew these
together end to end to make one long
strip of each kind of fabric. Then sew
all the strips together to make up the
cover. We made the finished width of
our strips 25cm (10in) (**Fig 1**) but of
course you can make them wider
bearing in mind the finished length
required. To finish, turn under and
hem about 2cm (1in) all around the
cover.

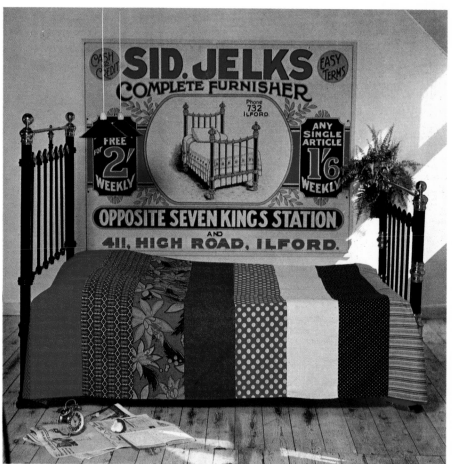

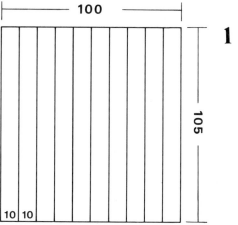

1

FUR FABRIC COVER
Finished size 252 × 168cm (99 × 66in)
(suitable for single bed)

Materials needed
*Fur fabric: 1.20m (1½yd) each in red
and white; 2.20m (2½yd) in beige; all
120cm wide (48 or 54in wide).
Cardboard for template.*

Fig 2 shows the color distribution for
the cover and also the size of the
finished triangles in the pattern. So
make up a cardboard template for the
triangle with two sides 30cm (12in)
long (this allows for a 1cm (½in) seam).
Use this template to cut accurately 27
red, 27 white and 54 beige triangles.
   Sew the triangles together in the
formation shown in **Fig 2** to make
twelve large squares (each one
comprising eight triangles) plus three
half squares. Then sew together the
squares and half squares—all oriented
the same way–to make the cover. Turn
under and stitch a small hem around
all four edges to finish.

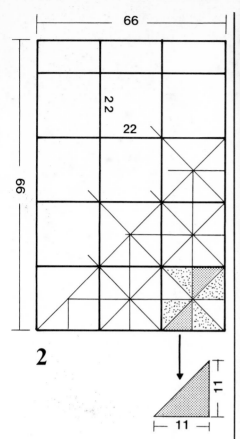

66

66

22

22

22

2

11

11

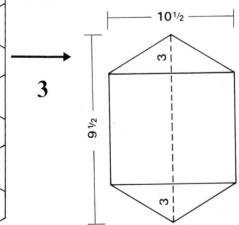

HEXAGONAL COVER
Finished size 226 × 162cm (90½ × 63in)
(suitable for single bed)

Materials needed
Fabric: about 4.30m (4¾yd)
   altogether–90cm wide (36in) or
   3.20m (3½yd)–120cm wide (48in)
Cardboard for template

Fig 3 shows the number of
hexagons used to make up this cover
and the finished size of a hexagon. On
the cardboard draw a hexagon exactly
this size and then add a 1cm (½in) seam
allowance all around and cut out a
card template that size. Use this
template to accurately mark and cut
your fabric hexagons, thirty-nine full
ones and six half hexagons (remember
to add a seam allowance on the long
edge of the half hexagons). Sew the
hexagons together in rows, sew the
rows together and hem the edges of the
cover.

63

90½

3

10½

3

9½

3

Hexagonal Cover – *instructions on page 97*

STAR COVER
Finished size 152 × 144cm (61 × 58in)
(suitable for single bed)

Materials needed
*Cotton fabric: about 6m–90cm wide
(7yd–36in) or 4.50m–120 cm wide
(5yd–48in)*
Cardboard for template

This makes a decorative throw-over for
a plain coverlet. It is made up of
twenty-five stars and **Fig 4** shows the
way they are put together and the size

of a finished star. On your cardboard draw a star exactly this large then add 1cm (½in) all round and cut your cardboard star that size. Use this template to mark and cut fifty fabric stars, some in a contrasting fabric if you like.

Sew the stars together in pairs, right sides facing, leaving a gap for turning. Turn right sides out, stitch closed the gaps and run a line of stitching right around each star to make the edges neat.

Now sew together the tips of sixteen stars in the pattern illustrated by the white stars in **Fig 4,** then sew on the remaining nine stars as indicated by the dark stars in **Fig 4.**

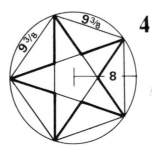

4

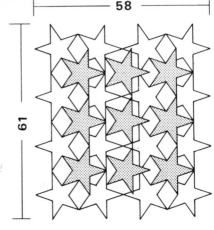

BRIGHTENING UP

Why not make a door really contribute to the decor? We have made doors a focus in the room—not just a way out! All you have to do is to decorate a board and then tack it to the door. You can easily change the design when you want to, or, if you move, take your "work of art" along with you. This is also the ideal solution if you're in rented accommodation and want to liven up a room quickly and cheaply, without causing damage. Of course, if you like, you can paint directly on the door.

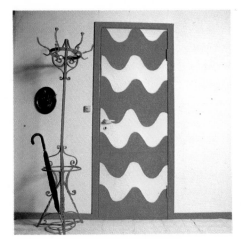

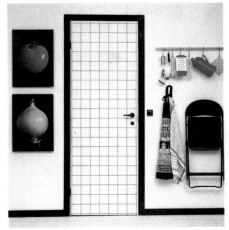

RED AND WHITE STRIPES
Simply give the door a coat of primer, draw on the outlines for the wavy stripes and paint them in. Paint the door surround and skirting board to match if you like.

PHOTOGRAPHS
Why not have a favorite photograph enlarged for your door? Take the picture to a photographic studio and ask them whether it will successfully enlarge to the size you want.

To mount the enlargement, dampen it and leave for fifteen minutes. (Draw key marks on the board if you like to help you place the photograph.) Then brush adhesive on the board (you can use wallpaper paste), lay on the photograph and, using a wet sponge, smooth it on the board working from the center outwards. As a finishing touch give the photograph a coat of clear varnish.

TILES
For this door treatment use a sheet of enamelled hardboard or laminated board with a tiled surface pattern—the sort often used for kitchen or bathroom panelling. Cut the sheet to size and stick on the hardboard using wood adhesive. Remember to roughen the surface of the hardboard to provide a good base.

Finish around the edges with one of the plastic edge-sealing strips sold specially for work with tiled surfaces. Mount the board.

BEAUTIFUL GIRLS
Not everybody is artistic, and drawing on a large scale can be tricky. So here's an easy way of transferring a design to your walls and door. Have a color slide made of a drawing or design you particularly like, then project it on the door. Trace over the projected image lightly in pencil and afterwards paint in the design.

General note

The type of board we used for our decorations is the slightly thicker kind of hardboard with an oiled surface. Try to get your lumber yard to cut it to the size you want; otherwise cut it with a fine-toothed saw.

If the board is to be fixed on the side of the door opposite the hinge, have the board cut about 1cm (½in) smaller all round than the actual door size, to clear the door surrounds. Mark the points for the handle and keyhole and drill holes for both.

Sand the edges of the board well and prepare the surface with primer before painting or papering on it. Roughen the surface by sanding to provide a key before gluing directly on to the board.

To mount the board, remove the handle and keyhole fitting on the door and secure the board with several tacks or a screw at each corner. Then fix the handle and keyhole fittings back in place.

WALLPAPER

Papering is probably the easiest and quickest way of decorating a door. Apply the paper to your board using wallpaper paste (following the manufacturer's instructions for use). Smooth the paper down on the board, working from the center outwards to squeeze out any air bubbles. Allow the paper to dry, then stick the edges of it around the sides of the board.

If you can manage to get hold of self-adhesive wallpaper the job is even easier. Just damp it, leave for fifteen minutes, then smooth down as before using a wet sponge.

BULLETIN BOARD

For this you need two pieces of board–the oiled hardboard plus a piece of insulation board for the notice board section. Ours measured 174 × 57cm (68½ × 22½in). Round the corners on the insulation board using a plate to mark the cutting lines and cut with a knife or a coping saw.

Prime and then paint the hardboard with glossy paint. Cover the insulation board with fabric (we used brown felt) taking it around the edges of the board and fixing to the back with staples.

Secure the bulletin board to the middle of the hardboard by screwing through the back of the hardboard, then mount the whole panel on the door (**Fig 1**).

1

22½

68½

CLOUD FABRIC

Paint your board with white primer first, otherwise the dark background of the board may show through the lighter parts of the fabric. We used a cloud fabric but any large interesting print that tones with your decor would do. Allow 5cm (2in) extra on each edge of the fabric for sticking down round the edges of the board.

Brush an even coat of adhesive on the board (we used diluted synthetic resin). Dampen the fabric and lay on the board. Smooth it down well, working from the middle outwards and making sure there are no air bubbles. When the glue is dry, stick the edges of the fabric around the sides of the board and onto the back. Give the fabric three or four coats of cellulose varnish, and for a smooth finish lightly sand the next to last coat. It is a good idea to try out the effect of the varnish on a small piece of fabric first.

DOLL DESIGN

Have a look at the design shown in **Fig 3.** Give the hardboard a coat of white primer and when dry mark it into squares then draw in the design in pencil. Paint in the colors separately, leaving each one to dry throughly before filling in the next. When finished, tack the board to the door (about 10 tacks) or screw it on (one small screw at each corner).

RED PANELLED DOOR

Prime your board carefully. Then cut the three frames shown in **Fig 2** from wooden batten 4.4cm (1¾in) wide by 9mm (⅜in) thick. Mark the positions for the frames on the board then stick them on with a good wood adhesive. Also pin through into them from the back of the board.

Give the frames a coat of primer, then paint the board and frames using two or three coats of gloss paint. Mount the board.

2

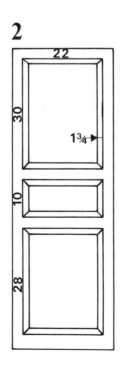

3

BAMBOO

To cover this door we used a bamboo blind. Cut the blind down to fit your board and stick it on using a wood adhesive. Mount the board on the door **(Fig 4).**

RAINBOW STRIPES

Prime the board and mark out the stripes on it in pencil **(Fig 5).** Colour each stripe separately leaving each one to dry before painting in the next. To make sure you get good straight lines you can mask one side of the line with masking tape before painting. Mark the corners clearly using a plate and paint these carefully by eye. Mount the board.

4

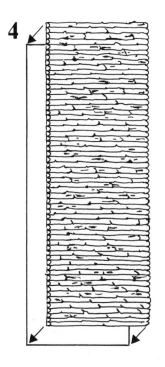

5

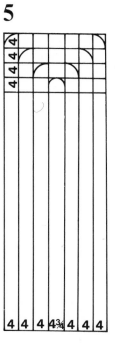

GRANDMA'S LAMPSHADES

'Old fashioned' in the nicest possible way, some delightfully 20's-looking with lots of lovely long fringing, these are shades that look elegant and interesting. We used fabrics to set off the beautiful curvy shapes of the frames–plush velour, sophisticated chiffon, pretty chintzy cottons and pure white broderie anglaise. Scout around to find frames roughly similar, either new or second hand, because half the attraction is their charming shape. See General note page 110 for method of binding wire frames.

PINK FRINGED SHADE

Materials needed
Flowered cotton fabric
Burlap for pattern
Binding tape
Wire frame (8-rib, see photograph)

Bind the frame (**Fig 2**) then make up a pattern piece for the frame as follows. Cut a piece of burlap on the bias large enough to easily cover two sections on the frame. Pin the center of the burlap to the middle rib of the two sections and secure to the other ribs with a few pins (**Fig 1a**–the arrow indicates the thread direction of the fabric). Then work to pull the fabric taut over the two sections securing with pins at 1cm ($\frac{1}{2}$in) intervals (**Fig 1b**). Mark on the burlap the exact positions of the outer ribs that enclose the two sections and unpin it from the frame. The lines you have just drawn are the fitting lines or seam lines for the pattern pieces. Cut the burlap down to within 2cm ($\frac{3}{4}$in) of the fitting lines all around and use this pattern to cut four identical pieces in the floral fabric. Cut these on the bias too.

Sew these pieces together to make the cover using a narrow French seam. To do this place the pieces wrong sides facing and machine stitch together just outside the fitting line (**Fig 3a**). Trim close to this stitching then fold back the fabric and stitch along the fitting line so the raw edges are enclosed (**Fig 3b**). This makes a neat seam on the inside of the cover.

Press the seams flat then pull the cover carefully over the frame and adjust it so that the seams lie over the ribs. Pin to the horizontal ribs so the cover is held taut over the frame. Sew to the top, center and bottom ribs with a line of small hemming stitches, then turn back the bottom edge of the fabric and stitch again (**Fig 6**). Trim off any excess fabric close to the stitching.

To cover the top edge sew up a tube or roll of fabric and stitch over the top edge. Finish the bottom with fringing. Sew on another roll of fabric to the other horizontal ring (see photograph).

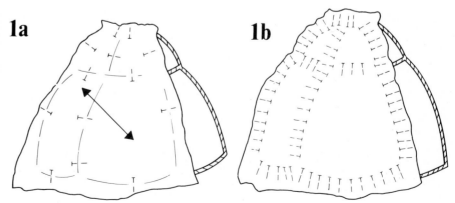

1a

1b

General note

For each of the lampshades you will need to bind the wire frame to make a foundation to which the cover can be stitched. Use either the special lampshade tape or if you need a particular color use seam binding. You need roughly twice as much tape as the length of frame to be bound.

Bind each vertical rib first, securing the end of the binding at the top as shown in **Fig 2a**. Then bind down to the bottom of the rib with the binding overlapping at quite an angle and pulled really tight–if it's slack it will turn when you try to stitch on it. At the base of the rib knot the binding tightly around the bottom ring as in **Fig 2b**. Bind all the vertical ribs like this then the top and bottom rings plus any horizontal ribs. These should be bound in one, taking the binding in a figure of eight (**Fig 2c**) around the vertical ribs. Finish off by knotting and stitching around one of the vertical ribs.

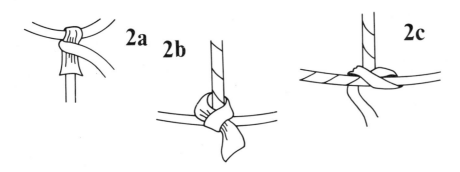

RUST VELOUR SHADE

Bind the frame and cover it exactly as for the Brown Chiffon shade (page 112) stitching the velour directly to the frame. Add a roll of velour to cover the top of the shade and the horizontal ribs. Finish the bottom edge with a matching fringe.

POM POM SHADE
Materials needed

Cotton fabric
Burlap for pattern
Four pom poms
*Hemispherical wire frame (see
  photograph)*

Bind the frame. Then pin a diamond of
burlap to the ribs so that it covers a
quarter of the frame (**Fig 4a**). Mark the
pinned rib positions and unpin from
the frame. Lay out flat and mark the
hanging corner (**Fig 4b**)–the length XY
should equal the height of the frame.

    Trim down the burlap to give a
pattern piece 2cm ($\frac{3}{4}$in) larger all
around then the marked outline or
fitting line. Cut four fabric pieces this
size and sew them together using the
French seam method explained for the
Pink Fringed Shade (page 109). Turn
under and sew a neat small hem along
the raw edges on the hanging corners
then stitch on the pom poms.

    Fit the cover over the shade, pinning
top and bottom, stitch firmly to the top
and lightly to the bottom ring. Add a
roll of fabric to finish the top of the
shade.

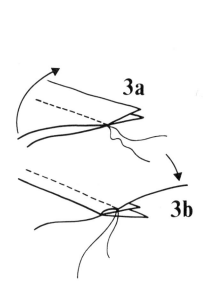

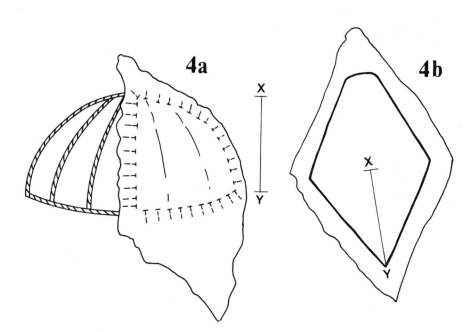

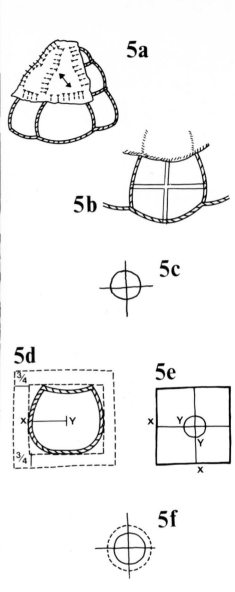

5a

5b

5c

5d

5e

5f

5g

5h

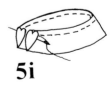

5i

BROWN CHIFFON SHADE

Materials needed
Chiffon fabric
Binding tape to match color of fabric
Braid and fringing to match
Wire frame (see photograph)

Unlike the other frames where the covers are machine stitched together then fitted over the frame, the fabric for this one is fitted and stitched directly on to the frame.

Bind the frame, then cut a piece of chiffon (on the bias) about 2cm (¾in) larger all around than a quarter of the upper frame. Use a few pins first of all to center the fabric over the ribs then pin taut with pins at 1cm (in) intervals (**Fig 5a**). Stitch the fabric to the ribs with small neat hemming stitches. Cut three more similar pieces of chiffon and sew on in the same way but turning in a small hem over the ribs that already have fabric stitched to them. Now trim away the excess fabric along the vertical ribs.

Making the sunray sections
Mark the center of each section in which the sunray pattern is to appear with a cross of tape attached to the ribs (**Fig 5b**). This will help in centering the design later.

To make up a paper pattern, work as follows. In the center of a large piece of paper draw a cross. Then draw in a circle whose diameter is one sixth the circumference of the section to be covered–work this out by measuring around the enclosing ribs, e.g. if the circumference of the ribs is 60cm (24in), the circle on the paper should be 10cm (4in) in diameter (**Fig 5c**).

To work out the overall size for the pattern look at **Fig 5d** and measure the distance XY on your lampshade (i.e. from the center of the section to its outermost point plus 2cm (¾in). Using this measurement draw in the square shown in **Fig 5e** on your paper. Cut the paper down to this size.

Cut a piece of chiffon and pin it to the corners of the paper pattern. Then using the pattern lines that you can see through the fabric as a guide, tack a cross on the fabric. Using double thread also sew a ring of gathering stitches 5mm ($\frac{1}{4}$in) outside the circle. (**Fig 5f**). Make the stitches 5mm ($\frac{1}{4}$in) on the front surface of the fabric and 1mm long on the reverse. This will ensure that the gathering looks less bulky on the front of the fabric, and this should be the side that shows when the fabric is stitched to the lampshade. Cut a hole 5mm ($\frac{1}{4}$in) inside the stitching and also cut the chiffon down to the pattern size.

Pull up the stitching to gather the fabric (**Fig 5g**) and tie off the thread firmly–there is quite a pull across the chiffon once it is stitched to the frame.

Pin the fabric over the frame section so the hole lies over the center of the tape cross, and so that the tape and thread crosses are aligned. Distribute the gathers evenly so they form the four sets of rays, then pin the fabric tightly over the frame with pins at 1cm ($\frac{1}{2}$in) intervals (**Fig 5h**). Sew the fabric to the ribs as you did for the upper parts of the cover. Make up and add the other sunray sections.

To cover each gathered center make a rose of chiffon. Cut a piece of fabric 12 × 4cm (5 × 1$\frac{1}{2}$in) and fold it in half lengthways. Turn in 5mm ($\frac{1}{4}$in) on the long raw edges and sew them together with gathering stitches in double thread (**Fig 5i**). Sew the ends of the strip together then pull up the gathering stitches to draw the fabric into a 'rose'. Sew a rose neatly over each of the sunray centers.

Pin on braiding to all the vertical ribs and sew on with zig-zag stitches made through the rib binding and from edge to edge across the back of the braid. Sew on the bottom fringing then finish all horizontal ribs plus the bottom edge with braiding.

BRODERIE ANGLAISE SHADE

Materials needed
Broderie anglaise fabric
*Broderie anglaise trim for frill and
    flowers*
Binding tape
Wire frame (8-rib see photograph)

Bind the frame and make a pattern piece in burlap to cover a quarter of the frame (see method given for pattern making in Pink Fringed Shade, page 109). Stitch the cover pieces together right sides facing and neaten the seams by zig-zag stitching and trimming.

Fit the cover and stitch to the top and bottom rings (see **Fig 6**). Gather a frill of the broderie anglaise trim and sew to the bottom edge, and make a roll of the fabric to finish the top ring.

To make the flowers that decorate the middle of each section cut 25cm (10in) lengths of the trim. Coil each length to make a "flower" and stitch to hold the coil together. Sew each flower carefully to the lampshade with fine stitches.

6

Once you start covering things with fabric you'll find it hard to stop! The more that matches the better the effect. The outlay is minimal–just 50cm (½yd) of fabric will do for a lot of small items–and the technique involved is so simple. We covered a range of objects centered around a desk, but dull-looking kitchen or bathroom things that receive the treatment too instantly look more exciting. Using a pretty floral fabric with a small pattern makes it very hard to spot the seams.

Materials needed
Cotton fabric with small pattern
Synthetic resin adhesive
Sharp craft knife and scissors
Varnish

General method
Basically our method is to saturate the fabric with adhesive which not only sticks it to the required surface but dries into it, making the fabric as easy to cut as paper–no frayed edges and good clean cuts. Finish with a coat of varnish which further binds the fabric and seals the raw edges and you have an easy-clean, durable surface.

For all articles to be covered use the following method. Draw the outline of the object to be covered on the wrong side of the fabric. Then cut the fabric an inch or so larger than this outline. Apply a thin coat of the diluted adhesive to the back of the fabric with a glue brush. (If you are going to cover a smooth surface like plastic, sand the surface well first to provide a base for the adhesive.)

Smooth the fabric over the article then brush on an even layer of adhesive all over the front of the fabric. Make sure at this stage that the fabric is pulled evenly over the article with no air bubbles.

Leave the adhesive to dry completely, by which time the fabric will be as crisp as paper and easy to cut. Then use either a sharp craft knife or scissors, as appropriate, and trim the fabric to fit the covered surface. Give the fabric-covered surfaces a coat of varnish.

FLOWER POT COVERS

These look very pretty and are simple to make since they just consist of a tube of cardboard a little larger than the height and circumference of the flower pot. The tube can be made from an oblong of cardboard stuck or stapled together.

Cover the cardboard tube with one piece of fabric, turning in and sticking about 5cm (2in) at either end to the inside of the tube. Square covers can be made using cardboard boxes–to negotiate the corners on these cut a

small V at each corner (**Fig 1**) and stick the flaps so formed to the inside edges of the box.

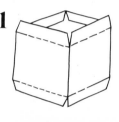
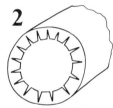

VASE

For a square vase use a waterproof container like a milk or fruit juice carton. Cut the top of the container off level using a sharp craft knife. Cut Vs into the corners as for the Flower Pot Covers and stick the flaps to the inside upper edge and to the base of the carton. To get the fabric to sit neatly around the base of a circular container, cut Vs as in **Fig 2** and stick the flaps to the bottom of the container.

BOXES

Any small box that's an interesting shape, like a French cheese box, can be covered to make a pretty holder for small items like jewelry, stamps, paper clips etc. Cover the whole box, or just the top. If the base is wood, give the wood a coat of varnish too.

TRAY

We covered an old scratched metal tray to give it new life and made a couple of napkins to match. Cut a circle of fabric to go inside the tray plus a strip of fabric wide enough to cover the inner and outer edges and fold under the base of the tray. Cut V's to make flaps that can be neatly stuck to the underside of the tray.

MATCHBOXES

If you cover one of the large economy boxes of matches it makes a very presentable matchholder for the table.

CIGARETTE OR PENCIL HOLDERS

For these we used sections cut from cardboard tubes. You can use the type used for mailing posters–these often have plastic caps for the ends which could be used as bases for the containers. If not you can make up a circular base with flaps to fit the inner diameter of the tube or, if the cardboard is fairly thick, just stick on a circle of cardboard. Cover the holders with fabric as for the circular vase.

BLOTTING PAD

Use a piece of thick cardboard for the pad–ours measured 48 × 35cm (19 × 14in). Cover this with plain fabric. To make each corner, simply cut a triangle of cardboard (with two sides approximately 9.5cm (3¾in) and cover with fabric, leaving a small border all around. When the adhesive is dry trim the fabric down to the size of the triangle. Give all four corners a coat of varnish, then fix to the pad by stapling.

FILE BOX

Cardboard file boxes quickly become tattered but can easily be rejuvenated with a pretty fabric covering. Press the fabric well into the contours of the box.

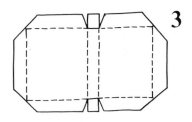

3

CHEAP FOLDERS

Cheap cardboard folders look attractive and become a good deal more hardwearing when covered with fabric. Lay the folder out flat and cover with fabric leaving a small border all around. When dry, trim the fabric level with the edge of the folder. Bend the folder closed and give it a coat of varnish.

GLASSES CASE

Dull plastic cases for glasses can be made to look quite special just by covering with fabric.

FOLDERS AND BOOKS

These are easy items to cover, especially the ring binders. For books, cover just as you would a school book, cutting a flap top and bottom (**Fig 3**) which can be pushed into the end of the spine. Mold the fabric round the book while it is shut and press it well into the spine grooves. Clip the corners before turning the flaps around the edges of the cover. For a paperback, trim the fabric flaps level with the spine when dry. Alternatively trim around the book level with the cover edges.

EASY & FUN

EASY & FUN

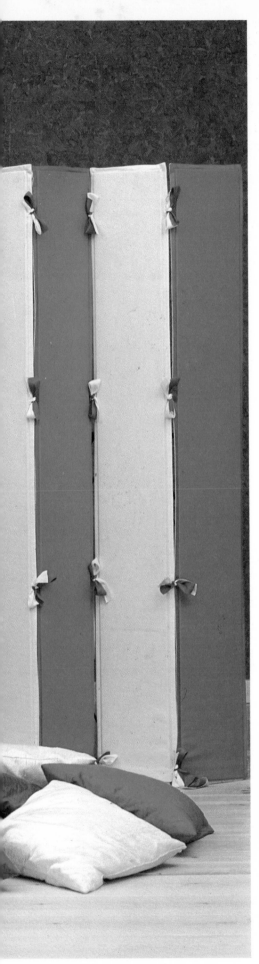

These screens are amazing. No nails, screws or hinges! And you can easily make one in an evening. They are basically a fabric cover divided into pockets each of which takes a chipboard panel. (Try to buy one of the lighter varieties, as standard chipboard is rather heavy.) The screens hinge because of the narrow gutters between each pocket.

They have a lot of advantages over more conventional screens. You can remove the covers for washing; you can use any material you like, matching your living room, kitchen or wherever; you can make them to any size; you can even use left over materials–and they are quick and cheap to make. (Remember to wash your fabric before sewing it, to prevent it shrinking when you wash it later.)

We made our screens in two different sizes: one with 4 wide panels and the other with 8 narrow panels.

General note

All the chipboard used for these screens is 12mm ($\frac{1}{2}$in) thick. We used just two sizes of board–A and B in **Fig 1**. It is best to have the boards cut to exactly these sizes by the lumber yard where you buy the board. Cutting them yourself without a bench and power tool could be difficult.

Before inserting the boards in the covers prepare them by smoothing off all edges really well with glasspaper. This will make them much easier to get into the covers. Where indicated round corners using a cup and pencil to mark the curve on the board, and cut it with a coping saw. Sand well.

When stitching the dividing lines to make the pockets in the covers always stitch in the same direction i.e. from the top of the cover downwards. This will prevent the fabric from puckering because it is being pulled in different directions by the stitching. The covers are a fairly tight fit over the boards so make sure you stitch the dividing lines as straight and evenly as possible. Draw round the boards on the covers to mark the stitching lines if you like.

GREEN AND WHITE REVERSIBLE SCREEN

Materials needed

Tough cotton fabric (we used gabardine)

Eight B-size boards

Tapes 15cm (6in) long: 48 white, 48 green

Cut sixteen pieces of fabric, eight green and eight white, each measuring 156 × 26cm ($62\frac{1}{2}$ × $10\frac{1}{2}$in). Turn up and stitch a 3cm (1in) hem at one end of each fabric piece— these will make the bottom edges of the cover.

Pin and tack the pieces together in pairs—one white and one green—with *right* sides facing. Then sew together round three sides allowing 1cm ($\frac{1}{2}$in) on the seam. Clip the two top corners (see **Fig 2a**) then turn right side out and press the edges well. Run a line of stitching around the three sides 1.5cm ($\frac{3}{4}$in) in from the edge.

Sew on the tapes at the intervals shown in **Fig 2b**. All but the two end boards will need tapes on both long edges. Note that the tapes are sewn on both surfaces of the boards and should

match the color of the side they are on. (**Fig 2b**).

Prepare the boards, fit them into the covers and pull the covers well down so the bottoms of the boards do not show. Then tie the panels together to make either of the combinations shown in the photographs on pages 120 and 121.

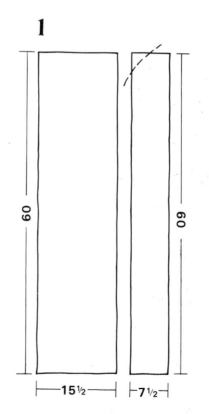

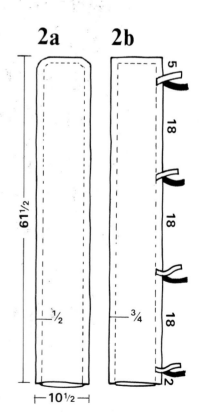

1   60   60   15½   7½

2a   61½   ½   10½

2b   5   18   18   ¾   18   2

PATCHWORK SCREEN
Materials needed

Cotton remnants for making patchwork,
(or printed patchwork fabric
176 × 154cm–70 × 61½in, i.e. 3.20m–90
or 120cm wide (3½yd–36 or 48in)
Cotton fabric 190 × 160cm (75 × 65in),
i.e. 3.80m–90cm wide (4yd–36in) or
3.20m–120cm wide (3½yd–48in) for
backing patchwork
Cotton fabric in complimentary
color/design for reverse of screen
176 × 154cm (70 × 61½in), i.e. 3.20m–90
or 120cm wide (3½yd–36 or 48in)
Edge-binding
Eight B-size boards (two with one
rounded corner)
Cardboard for patchwork template

We made up our own squared
patchwork fabric for one side of this
screen from several different patterned
fabrics in red. This patchwork was
designed to fit the screen such that the
width of each board is covered by two
squares of the patchwork.

If you want to make your own
patchwork too, cut a cardboard
template 12.7 × 12cm (5¼ × 5in) and
use it to cut 240 fabric squares. Tack
under a 1cm (½in) hem round each
square to reduce them to 10.7 × 10cm
(4¼ × 4in) squares. Sew these on to the
backing fabric to make a patchwork
rectangle. Note: sew this patchwork
centered on the backing.

Now cut the backing fabric down to
the width of the patches and on the
length leave about a 1cm (½in) edge at
the top and a 3cm (1in) edge of backing
at the bottom.

Hem up the 3cm (1in) of backing at
the base of the patchwork and also
hem up 3cm (1in) on one long edge of

the fabric you are using for the reverse
side of the screen. These hemmed edges
will make the bottom edges of the
screen cover. Pin the two halves of the
cover together wrong sides facing and
sew together around the edges allowing
1cm (½in) on the seam–round and trim
the upper corners, then bind the seam.

Next divide the cover up to make
eight 20cm pockets (8in) pockets
separated by 1.5cm (⅝in) gaps as in **Fig
3a.** To do this stitch either side of every
second column of patches as in **Fig 3b.**

This type of traditional patchwork
does take a little time to make up, so if
you don't have the time use a fabric
with a ready-printed patchwork design.
Or try a random patchwork design.

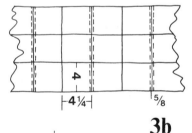

3b

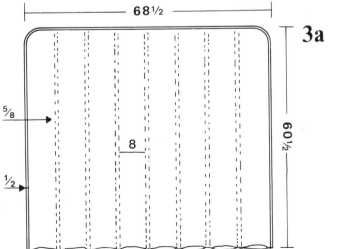

3a

KITCHEN SCREEN
Materials needed
*Oilcloth: two pieces 169 × 155cm
  (68 × 62in)*
Four A-size boards
Stick-on or screw-in kitchen hooks

This is an easy to clean screen made
entirely of oilcloth. On the long side of
each oilcloth piece turn up and sew a
3cm (1in) hem–these hems make the
bottom edges of the screen cover. Put
the pieces *wrong* sides together then
pin, tack and sew together around
three sides allowing 1.5cm ($\frac{3}{4}$in) on the
seam. Bind this seam with 3cm (1$\frac{1}{2}$in)
binding.

Divide the cover into four 40cm
(16in) pockets as for the Baby Screen
(**Fig 4**). Insert the boards then attach
the kitchen hooks.

BEDROOM SCREEN
Materials needed
*Quilted fabric: one piece 178 × 155cm
  (71 × 62in) i.e. 3.20m–90 or 120cm
  wide (3$\frac{1}{2}$yd–36 or 48in)*
*Cotton fabric: one piece same size as
  quilted fabric*
*Eight B-size boards (two with one
  rounded corner)*

One side of the screen cover is made in
quilted fabric and the other in ordinary
cotton. You can buy attractive ready-
quilted fabrics but if you're feeling
adventurous you could try quilting
your own.

Sew up a 3cm (1in) hem on one long
side of both the quilted and ordinary
fabric pieces (to make the bottom
edges of the screen cover). With *right*
sides facing, pin tack and sew the
pieces together around three sides
allowing 1cm ($\frac{1}{2}$in) on the seam.
(Round the upper corners using a cup
and pencil to mark the stitching line.
Trim the corners after stitching.) Turn
the cover right side out, press the edges
well then run a line of stitching around
the three sides 1cm ($\frac{1}{2}$in) from the edge.

Divide the cover into eight 20cm
(8in) pockets as for the Patchwork
Screen (**Fig 3**) and insert the boards.

BABY SCREEN

Materials needed
*Oilcloth: one piece 171 × 156cm
  (69 × 62$\frac{1}{2}$in)*
Cotton fabric: one piece as above
Four A-size boards
*Adhesive or suction hooks to hold baby
  things.*

On one long side of the oilcloth and the
cotton fabric piece turn up and sew
3cm (1in) hem (these edges will make
the bottom of the screen cover). With
the pieces *right* sides together pin, tack
and sew together around three sides
1cm ($\frac{1}{2}$in) in from the edge. Clip the
upper corners diagonally and turn the
cover right side out. Press the seam
well between your fingers (or use an
iron on the fabric side) then run a line
of stitching around the three sides
1.5cm ($\frac{3}{4}$in) in from the edge.

Divide the cover into four pockets
with the lines of stitching shown in
Fig 4. Insert the prepared boards and
on the oilcloth side of the screen stick
the hooks and pockets to hold all your
baby equipment.

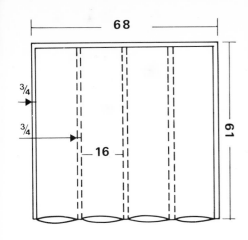

68

3/4

3/4

16

61

TEA COSIES

Cosies can come in all sorts of fun shapes and every kind of fabric. They are easy and quick to put together and make economical small presents. Have a look at the pictures of the ones we made up and see if they afford any inspiration. If you keep a remnants bag then have a rummage through, often a particular fabric will suggest a certain design. Use washable fabrics if possible plus good thick cotton wadding–it's worth checking too that any binding or appliquéd designs you add will wash too.

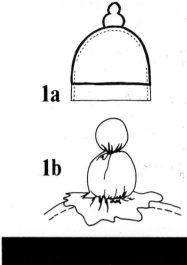

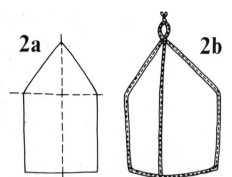

DOLL

Follow the general instructions for the Motorcar inner cosy (page 128), only cut the wadding the shape shown by the bold line in **Fig 1a** and the inner fabric the shape extended by the faint line. Sew these pieces together to make the inner cosy leaving gaps in the seam for spout and handle (**Fig 1a**). Bind the edges of the gaps with seam binding, and turn up the inner fabric cover round the bottom of the wadding and hem neatly.

To make up the doll's body, cover the wadding shape at the top of the inner cosy with a piece of pink fabric tied as shown in **Fig 1b**. Then sew on two arms made from tubes of fabric filled with strips of wadding. Make up a small blouse with long puff sleeves, slip on the doll and stitch at the waist. Add the skirt which effectively makes the outer cover–this should have gaps in the side seams for the spout and handle and needs to be hemmed level with the bottom of the cosy. Make up an apron with ties that cover all the stitching and gathering at the waist, then add the hair made from wool.

3-SIDED COSY

You can make this cosy from any patterned fabric. We just happened to find some bumble bee fabric which seemed to suit its hive shape.

Measure the circumference of your teapot including spout and handle. Be generous with your measurement. Divide this dimension by three to give the basic width for your pattern piece. Draw up a paper pattern this width plus 2.5cm (1in) either side and roughly the shape shown in **Fig 2a**–make the cosy what height you like. Also use this pattern to cut three pieces of wadding and three pieces of fabric to make up the inner cosy.

Then use the pattern to cut the outer cover pieces but allowing an extra 1cm (½in) on all sides except the bottom. Sew these pieces together wrong sides facing and bind the three seams but not along the bottom. Tie the ends of the binding into a loop at the top of the cosy. Slip this outer cover over the inner cosy and enclose all the bottom raw edges in a binding to finish (**Fig 2b**).

HOUSE

Measure your teapot and make up a four-sided cover from wadding roughly to the shape shown in **Fig 3a**. Make up a similar inner fabric cover to fit inside this, and an outer cover (4cm (1½in) longer) to fit over the wadding. Cut a slit in either end 'wall' through all of these layers for the spout and handle and bind the raw edges of the slits. Turn up the 4cm (1½in) on the outer cover and hem neatly inside the cosy.

Make up a felt roof to fit with scalloped edge and add all the other features (**Fig 3b**) made from felt and fabric scraps.

Basic materials for all cosies
Cotton fabric for outer cover
Tough cotton fabric for inner cover
Thick cotton wadding
Scraps of fabric for individual designs
Edge binding as appropriate

MOTORCAR

This cosy, like most of the others, is made up of three layers—a tough inner cover of cotton fabric, an outer cotton cover with a design stitched to it, and sandwiched between these two a wadding layer.

To work out the size for the cosy, measure your teapot from handle to spout across the widest part (see photograph) and also from top to bottom. Be a little generous with your measurements. Transfer these dimensions to a piece of stiff paper and on it draw your design outline to fit the measurements. Use this to cut your fabric pieces as follows.

For the inner fabric, and wadding layers add about 2cm (¾in) all round to the pattern outline, except along the base (see bold line in **Fig 4**), and cut

4

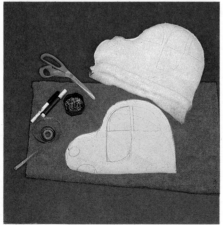

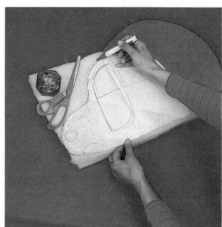

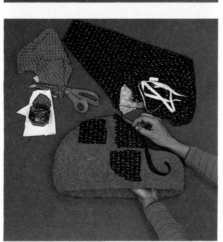

two pieces of wadding and two pieces of inner fabric that size. For the outer cover add about 3cm (1¼in) to the initial outline and 4cm (1½in) at the base (see broken line in **Fig 4**) and cut two pieces of fabric that size.

The inner cosy, comprising inner fabric and wadding, is sewn up as one operation. Put the inner fabric pieces right sides together and on either side pin the wadding. Tack and sew these four layers together (except along the base!) allowing 1cm (½in) on the seam.

Before you sew up the outer cover stitch on the car design to either or both pieces. Use scraps of fabric and felt to make up the windows, doors, wheels, etc., and to give the windows and doors a little bulk put a thin layer of wadding under them before you stitch them on.

Finally sew the two outer cover pieces together right sides facing (allowing 1cm (½in) on the seam) and turn right side out. Pull this cover over the inner cosy and hem up the bottom 4cm (1½in) inside the cosy.

PEAR

This is made in exactly the same way as the Motorcar cosy only pear-shaped. For each leaf cut two pieces of shiny green fabric 1cm (½in) larger than the required finished size. Sew a thin piece of wadding to the wrong side of one piece. Then pin and stitch the pieces together right sides facing leaving a small gap for turning. Turn right side out and stitch closed the gap. Run a line of stitching around the leaf edge and also stitch the vein pattern (see photograph). For the stalk, sew up a small tube of fabric, turn right side out, poke in some wadding to plump it out, sew up the ends and stitch to the cosy.

VELVET COSY

This is a satisfying way of making up a beautiful rainbow colored cosy. Just buy 3cm (1¼in) wide velvet ribbons in all colors and stitch them together to make up two pieces of fabric for an outer cover. Then make up the cosy following the general instructions given for the Motorcar.

COSY WITH POCKETS

The pockets on this cosy can hold two matching breakfast napkins. Cut and make up an inner cosy as for the Motorcar. Also cut the outer cover pieces. For the pocket cut an extra panel the same width and roughly half the total depth of the outer cover. Bind the upper edge of this panel then tack it to one of the cover pieces. Divide the pocket into two smaller ones with a line of stitching, and cover the stitching with binding (**Fig 5**).

Put the cover pieces *wrong* sides together and sew up allowing 1cm ($\frac{1}{2}$in) on the seam. Bind the seam edges, pull the cover over the inner cosy and hem up the bottom 4cm ($1\frac{1}{2}$in) inside the cosy—this bottom edge will of course include the pocket layer on one side.

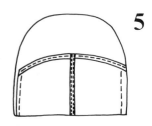

5

BOXING GLOVE

Have a look at the Motorcar cosy—this one is made up in the same way. Use several different patterned fabrics to make up a piece of patchwork large enough to give the two sides of the outer cover. Make the bottom 10cm (4in) of the outer cover sides from plain fabric, and sew a piece of binding over the seam where the plain fabric starts.

Make up the inner cosy. Then sew up the outer cover wrong sides together and bind around the raw edges. Pull the cover over the inner cosy and hem up the bottom 4cm ($1\frac{1}{2}$in) neatly inside the cosy leaving a band of plain fabric around the base of the glove (see **Fig 6**).

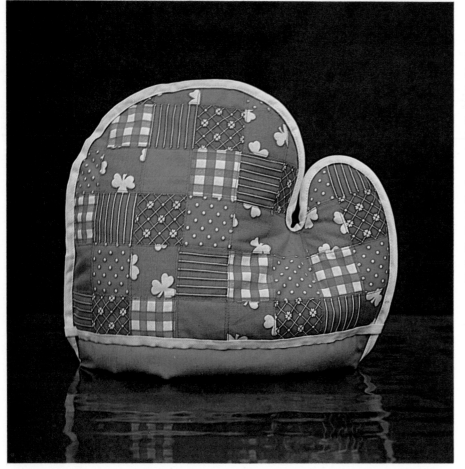

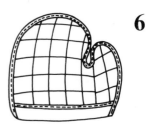

6

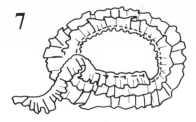

7

RUFFLED COSY

The ruffles on this cosy consist of different patterned lace and various pretty fabric frills. To make the fabric frills cut long lengths of cotton fabric and stitch a small neat hem along one edge. Just over 5mm ($\frac{1}{4}$in) in from the raw edge tack a line of running stitches and pull them up to gather the frill evenly. Gather the lengths of lace by the same method.

Make up an inner cosy the shape you want, as for the Motorcar, and also cut the two outer cover pieces. Take each outer cover piece and, starting from the outer edge and working inwards, pin and stitch on rings of lace and fabric frill so that each successive ring of lace or fabric covers the previous raw edge (**Fig 7**). When you've nearly reached the center, stitch on an oval of fabric to cover the last raw edges (see pink satin oval in photograph).

Place the two ruffled cover pieces right sides facing and pin together around the edges–as you do so include a length of gathered lace in the seam (the lace should lie towards the center of the fabric between the two layers so that it edges the seam when the cover is turned right side out). Sew up the cover and turn right side out.

Pull the cover over the inner cosy and hem up the 4cm ($1\frac{1}{2}$in) at the base to the inside of the cosy.

CAT

This cosy is made up in shiny silver fabric by exactly the same method as the Motorcar. **Fig 8** gives the general outline for the cat shape. Clip the seam on the outer cover well, before turning right side out.

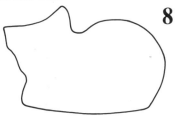

8

QUILTED KITCHEN IDEAS

How about a really cheap and simple way of brightening up your kitchen without all the fuss and expense of paints and wallpapers. You'll find here a whole range of delightful kitchen ideas that look attractive and are very useful.

We have made ours in a floral pattern, but you can use stripes, checks, dots or perhaps a plain fabric with a contrasting colored or patterned edging–it's up to you. We have included several kettle holders in various fabrics just to give you some idea of the possibilities.

Once you have got the hang of quilting you will find it is quite quick to do, and a set of two or three matching items makes a very welcome present.

Materials needed
Good washable cotton fabric (plain or
  patterned)
Washable cotton wadding
Edge binding
Sewing machine with quilting foot

General note
Most of the items in this sections involve a small amount of simple quilting, and while there are some quilting hints on pages 10–13, the general working method for these items is covered in the instructions for the Kettle Holder. Where the reverse side of the quilting will not show, e.g. in an oven glove or tea cosy, you can economize by using a cheaper cotton as the backing. In all cases where rounding of corners or cutting notches or circles within quilted panels is necessary, make up a quilted panel slightly larger than the required finished size first, *then* trim it down, cut notches and round corners etc.

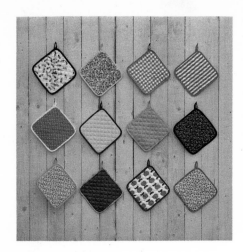

KETTLE HOLDER

Fig 1 shows the finished size of our large square kettle holder—the smaller one is 18cm (7in) square finished size.

For each kettle holder you will need two pieces of cotton fabric and a piece of cotton wadding, each cut 2cm ($\frac{3}{4}$in) larger all around than the required finished size. On the right side of one of the cotton pieces mark your quilting lines in chalk pencil—on this holder and other items these criss-cross diagonally at 3cm (1in) intervals (see top left photograph). Sandwich the wadding between the two cotton pieces, then carefully pin, tack and stitch through all layers, following the quilting lines. Stitch along all the lines running in the same direction, then along all the others.

Trim the holder to size—draw round a cup edge to give an accurate cutting line for the rounded corners. To finish the edges add the binding and fix a hanging loop at one corner.

2-IN-1 KETTLE HOLDER

This holder with its pocket at each end is also ideal for removing hot things from the oven. **Fig 2** shows the finished size of the holder, so cut your fabrics and wadding for the main piece and the two pockets a little larger all around. Quilt the main piece, and also the pocket pieces if you like.

Bind the straight edge on each pocket then pin, tack and stitch the pockets to the main piece. Trim close to the seam and add the edge binding.

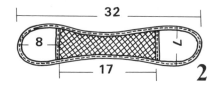

OVEN GLOVES

These oven gloves are specially made extra long to cover wrists and cuffs. **Fig 3** gives the pattern for a ladies (A) and a child's (B) glove. Pattern A also indicates the cut-off point for a conventional shorter glove. (To make a perfect fit, draw the outline of your hand plus 1cm ($\frac{1}{2}$in) on a piece of paper.)

Draw up the pattern to size and cut four pieces in cotton fabric (two reversed) and two in cotton wadding allowing 1cm ($\frac{1}{2}$in) all round for the seam. Make up and quilt the two identical halves of the glove then sew together. Trim close to the seam and turn the glove right side out. Finish the wrist edge with binding and add a hanging loop.

FRENCH BREAD HOLDER

This is made in two pieces—a quilted circular base and a quilted oblong panel (see **Fig 4** for finished quilted sizes). Sew the oblong into a cylinder by joining the short sides and turn right side out. Sew in the base (wrong sides facing) and bind the top and bottom raw edges. Add a hanging loop to the top edge. You can then keep your french bread hanging in its own holder on the wall.

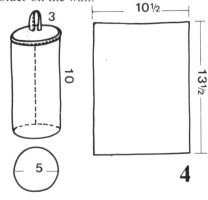

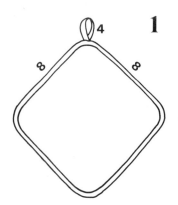

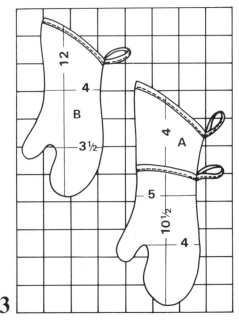

TEA COSY

This cosy will fit most sizes of tea pot–its finished size is 38cm wide by 29cm high (15 × 11in). It is made in two parts–an outer cotton cover and an inner cosy of extra thick cotton wadding.

Cut two pieces of wadding 36cm wide × 35cm high (14 × 13½in) and two pieces of cotton fabric 38cm wide × 36cm high (15 × 14in). Trim the upper corners on each piece as shown in **Fig 5**.

Pin tack and sew the wadding pieces together to make the inner cosy. Then sew the cotton pieces together (wrong sides facing) and finish all the edges with binding. Pull the cover over the wadding cosy then turn up the bottom 7cm (3in) of the cover and slipstitch to the inside of the cosy.

Of course, your tea pot may be a quite different size, but you can easily adapt the measurements to suit your pot.

TIE-ON COSY

This type of cosy can stay on the pot while you pour. It is made up of two identical quilted halves shaped to fit the curve of the tea pot. **Fig 6** gives the pattern for one half.

Draw up the pattern to size and cut four pieces of cotton fabric (two reversed) and two in wadding. Quilt the two halves of the cosy and in each half sew the three darts indicated by V's in **Fig 6**. Trim each dart close to the stitching. Sew the two cosy halves together (right sides facing) between points XY and PQ. Turn right side out, bind all raw edges and sew on the tape ties to each half as shown in **Fig 6**.

PLACE MAT

The finished size of the mat is 34 × 45cm (13 × 18in) and the corners are rounded as in **Fig 7** (inset in the diagram)–you can use a small plate to do this. Make up the mat as a quilted panel just like the Kettle Holder.

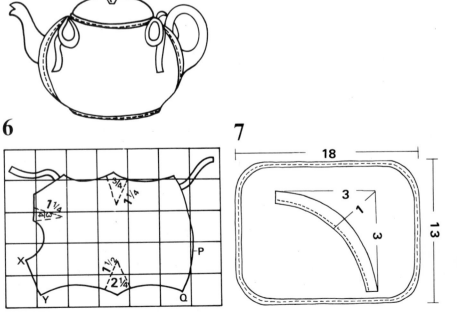

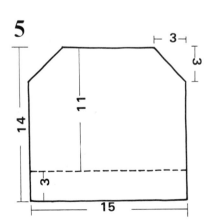

5

6

7

FRYING PAN GRIP

Some heavy cast-iron pans do not have insulated handles so a special quilted grip is a good idea. Make up a quilted panel that measures 17×14cm ($7 \times 5\frac{1}{2}$in) finished size. On one surface sew four pieces of elastic in the positions shown in **Fig 8**. Then sew together the two 17cm (7in) sides and turn the cylinder right side out (the elastic is now to the inside of the grip). Finish the raw edges with binding.

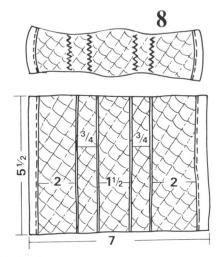

OBLONG LADLE HOLDER

Make up a quilted panel 13×34cm (5×13in) finished size, bind the edges and add three hanging loops (**Fig 9**).

Make the elasticated strip which actually holds the utensils as follows. You need 30cm (12in) of 2cm (1in) wide elastic. To cover this make up a tube of cotton fabric about 20cm (8in) longer than the elastic. Slip the tube over the elastic, gather evenly and pin. Zig-zag stitch through the elastic to hold the gathers and neatly hem the fabric over the ends of the elastic.

Stitch this elasticated strip to the center of the quilted panel to make six 5cm (2in) pockets (**Fig 9**). For strength use a double row of stitching at each fixing point.

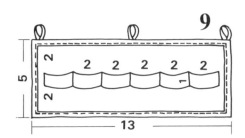

SQUARE LADLE HOLDER

The rings used for this holder are plain wooden curtain rings which can be wrapped with edge binding, stained or painted to match the rest of the holder.

Make up the square quilted panel to the finished size shown in **Fig 10**. To attach the rings cut a tiny hole in the quilted panel just above each ring position, loop a piece of edge binding round each ring and poke the ends through the holes. Hand sew the ends firmly to the back of the panel to secure the rings.

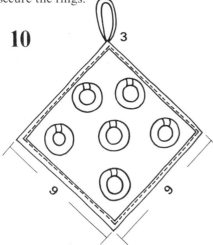

STEW POT COVER

This type of cover is ideal for the straight-sided kind of casserole or stew pot. The cosy consists of a quilted base and a quilted panel to fit the height and circumference of the pot–so scale the pattern up or down to fit your own particular pot. **Fig 11** shows the size cover we made.

Quilt the base and panel and in the latter cut the handle notches shown in **Fig 11**. Bind the edges of the notches and also along the straight edges on that side, extending the tapes to make ties (**Fig 11**).

Sew the panel into a cylinder by joining the short sides, sew in the base and turn the cover right side out. Slip over the stew pot and tie the tapes above the handles.

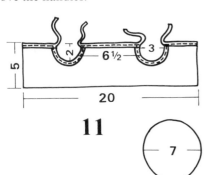

CRISPBREAD HOLDER AND COVER

This type of holder and cover is suitable for the large round Scandinavian type crispbreads that have a hole in the middle. The holder consists of a circle of plywood a little larger than the crispbread with a piece of wooden dowel screwed to the center of it (**Fig 12a**).

The cover consists of two quilted pieces–an oblong and a circular top with a hole cut in the middle (see **Fig 12b** for sizes). Stitch the oblong into a cylinder by joining the short sides. Bind the edge of the hole in the top piece and sew into the cylinder. Turn the cover right side out and bind the remaining raw edge. (**Fig 12b**).

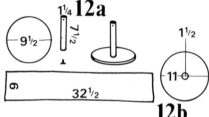

CHAIR COVERS

Measure the size of your chair seat and make up a quilted panel to fit the top of it with ties to hold the panel to the side or back struts of the chair.

For the back cover again measure your chair and make up a quilted 'cosy type' cover that will fit snugly over the chair back. **Fig 13** shows the finished size and shape of our two covers.

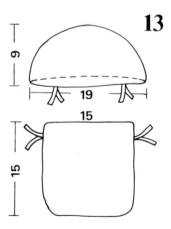

COOKING SCARF

This really is a useful thing to have around if you've just washed your hair and don't want it to smell of cooking! Cut one large triangle of cotton fabric (**Fig 14**) then add wadding and an extra piece of fabric to make the quilted panel at the front. Finish the edges with binding.

CHILD'S APRON

This tabard-style apron is very simple to make and a good cover-up for children. Our pattern (**Fig 15**) is suitable for a six-year-old so scale the pattern up for larger sizes.

Draw up the pattern to size and cut the main apron piece. Cut the oval for the head then bind the edges of the oval and all around the edges of the apron. Make up the tie, also with bound edges, and stitch across the back of the apron at waist level. (The ends tie around the front of the waist as shown in the photograph.) To finish, cut the pocket piece, bind the edges and sew to the front of the apron.

LADIES' APRON

Our apron is a medium size—see **Fig 16** for pattern. Cut the main apron piece then quilt just the top 12cm (5in) using another piece of cotton and some wadding cut to the same outline as the apron top. Bind all around the edge of the apron, add the neck strap and waist ties.

Cut the pocket as one piece, sew on two strips of binding at the points where the pocket will be subdivided and then bind the edges. Make the three-slot holder from a strip of petersham covered with cotton fabric.

Sew the pocket on to the apron then divide into three smaller pockets with lines of stitching either side of the dividing strips.

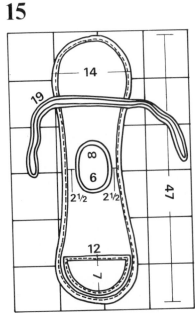

15

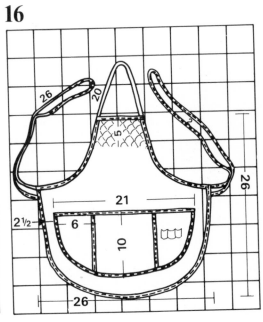

16

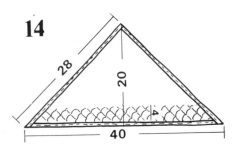

14

These wall tidies are charmingly and amusingly decorative, but they are also practical. They are an excellent way of storing all those odds and ends that tend to sit around on desks and table tops.

They are all made basically from a fabric backing onto which the pockets are sewn, strengthened with wooden battens at top and bottom to make the holder hang properly.

The best way to design a holder to suit your needs is to lay a large piece of paper on the floor, place all the objects you want to keep in the tidy on top of it and arrange them in the most suitable groups. Then you draw rough pocket outlines around them to give you paper patterns for the pockets.

Children will love keeping their toys in the strong holder with the cartoon characters.

General note

To hang the tidies, drill a couple of holes in the top batten or wooden frame to take screw fittings, a cord or wall hooks.

The blind fabric we refer to is the specially stiffened fabric sold by some large stores for home window-blind making. This hangs well and of course the cut edges won't fray.

DOLL DESIGN

Finished size 110 × 90cm (44 × 36in)

Materials needed

Blind fabric: one piece 125 × 90cm
(49 × 36in)
Fabric remnants for doll design and
pockets
Lining fabric for pockets
Elastic for pencil holders
Wooden dowel: two 3cm (1in) diameter
pieces, 90cm (36in) long

Use the pattern given in **Fig 1** to cut the fabric pieces for the doll's dress, body, boots and hair. If you use fabrics that fray, cut the fabric pieces 1cm ($\frac{1}{2}$in) larger all around, then tack under a 1cm ($\frac{1}{2}$in) hem all around, press well and appliqué to the blind fabric backing (see photograph). Make sure the doll is centered on the backing.

Then pin paper pockets on the doll, perhaps with samples of the different fabrics on them (see photograph) so you have some idea what the finished design will look like. Try drawing the face on a piece of tracing paper too.

For each pocket cut two identical pieces of fabric–one from the fabric you've chosen to use and one lining piece. Cut them 1–2cm ($\frac{1}{2}$–1in) wider at the top than at the bottom to allow more room at the mouth of the pocket. Pin and sew the two pieces together *right* sides facing and stitch together leaving a gap for turning on one side. Turn the pocket right side out, hem the opening closed and press the pocket well. Then pin and sew in position. This method will make a neat strong pocket.

Add all the pockets and holders, put the bows on the pigtails and draw on

the face with black marking pen–alternatively embroider the features.

Finally sew a hem at either end of the blind fabric deep enough to take the 3cm (1in) wooden dowel. The finished length of the tidy should be about 110cm (44in).

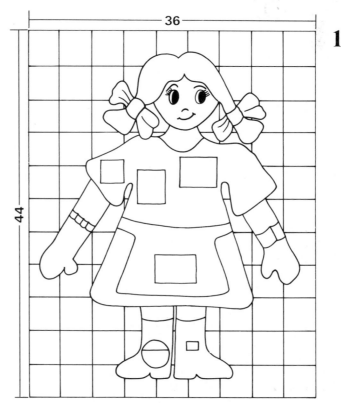

1

CHILDREN'S OILCLOTH TIDY
Finished size 110 × 90cm (43 × 36in)

Materials needed
Oilcloth: one piece 114 × 90cm
(45 × 36in); several pieces for pockets
Clear plastic: small piece for pocket
window
Stick-on cartoon characters
Edge binding
Wooden batten: two pieces 4 × 1cm,
90cm long (1½ × ½in, 36in long)
Polyurethane varnish, and adhesive.

The cartoon characters really make this
tidy. Ideally they can be cut from any
plastic cloth on which they are printed.
They could be transfers, or even cut
from a comic and covered with
adhesive plastic film. For the pockets
and backing we used oilcloth since it is
easy to wipe sticky fingermarks off it.

Fold over and pin about 7cm (3in) at
either end of the long piece of oilcloth
and use a cup and ball-point pen to
mark the semicircular cut-outs (**Fig 2**).
Cut through the double thickness at
either end, unpin the folds and bind the
edges of the cut-out ovals. Also bind

the long sides of the oilcloth. Fold over
and pin 7cm (3in) at either end again
and sew a hem deep enough to take the
battens.

Cut the pockets the size you want,
allowing an extra 1–2cm (½–1in) on the
width at the top of each. Bind the edges
of each pocket then pin and stitch to
the oilcloth backing. Cut flaps for some
of the pockets if you like, bind the
edges and sew in position about 1cm
(½in) above the pocket edge. To make it
easy to see what's inside the large
pocket we stitched in a window of clear
plastic.

Sand the ends of the battens and
drill holes (**Fig 2**) to take screws, hooks
or a hanging cord. Give them a coat or
two of polyurethane varnish and insert
in the top and bottom hems. Finally
decorate the tidy by sticking on your
cartoon characters.

2

36

43

PICTURE FRAME

Materials needed

Old picture frame
Plywood to fit back of frame
Tough fabric (e.g. blind fabric) to make
*   cover for plywood*
Cotton fabrics plus lining fabric for
*   pockets*

The idea behind this tidy is quite
simple–you make a tough cover to go
over the piece of plywood. This fits into
the back of the frame and is held in
with tacks just like a normal picture
back.

Cut the plywood to fit the back of
the frame–it should not fit too tightly.
On one half of the cover mark the
inner outline of the picture frame.
Make up pockets and holders as for
the Doll Design (page 141) and sew to
the cover within the marked outline.
Stitch up the cover around three sides,

slip in the plywood then slipstitch the
cover closed along its fourth side. (The
cover should be a tight fit over the
plywood.) Fit the completed panel in
the picture frame and secure with
tacks.

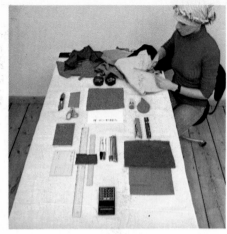

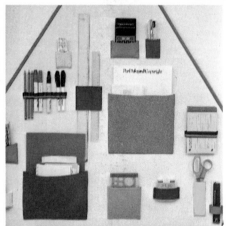

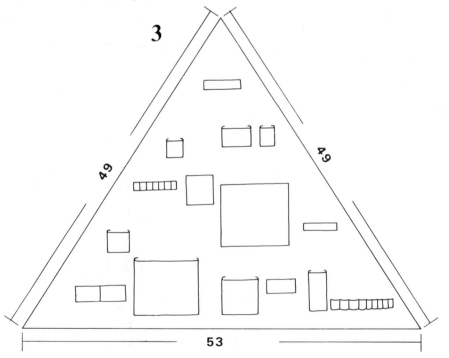

MINI OFFICE

Finished size approximately
125 × 125 × 135cm (49 × 49 × 53in)

Materials needed

*Tough cotton fabric: 1.5m × 1.5m
(59 × 59in) wide*
Cotton fabrics and lining for pockets
Elastic for holders
*Wooden batten 2.5cm (1in) square: two
pieces 125cm (49in); one piece 135cm
(53in)*
*Wooden batten 2 × 0.5cm ($\frac{3}{4} \times \frac{1}{4}$in): two
pieces 125cm (49in); one piece 135cm
(53in)*
Hammer and tacks, or staple gun

Use the 2.5cm (1in) square batten to
make up a triangular frame. On the
piece of tough cotton fabric mark the
outline of the frame in chalk pencil
plus the pocket positions (**Fig 3**). Make
up the pockets and holders as for the
Doll Design (page 141)–remember to
make them 1–2cm ($\frac{1}{2}$–1in) wider at the
top–and sew to the cotton backing.

Cut the backing down to about 7cm
(3in) larger all round than the frame.
Lay the backing panel over the frame,
pull the edges round it and tack or
staple them to the back of the frame so
that the fabric is held taut.

To finish, paint the 2 × 0.5cm
($\frac{3}{4} \times \frac{1}{4}$in) batten a color to suit the tidy
and tack it around the front edges of
the frame (see photograph).

3

49

49

53

144

MAGAZINE RACK
Finished size 104 × 30cm (41 × 12in)

Materials needed
Blind fabric or heavy cotton: backing
*   piece 120 × 30cm (47 × 12in); five*
*   pockets 21 × 30cm (8½ × 12in)*
Edge binding
Wooden batten: one piece 6 × 1cm and
*   30cm long (2 × ½ × 12in) one piece*
*   2.5 × 1cm and 30cm long*
*   (1 × ½ × 12in)*

Bind the edges of the piece of backing
fabric, then sew a hem at the top to
take the 6cm (2in) batten and one at
the bottom for the 2.5cm (1in) batten.
The finished length should be about
104cm (41in).

Round the upper corners on the five
pocket pieces. Turn under and sew a
1cm (½in) hem along the bottom of
each piece, then bind the remaining
raw edges.

Pin and sew the bottom of the lowest
pocket to the backing just above the
lower hem. Also catch in this seam the
ends of two straps to make a paper
holder–these can be strips of wide
colored elastic or made up from scraps
of blind fabric with bound edges (see
photograph). Cut two slits near the top
of the pocket flap, poke the other ends
of the straps through (**Fig 4a**) and sew
to the back of the flap.

Pin and stitch the next pocket in
position so that its base is hidden by
the upper edge of the bottom
pocket–note that just the bottoms of
the pockets are sewn to the backing at
this stage. When all the pockets are in
position like this (**Fig 4b**) sew them to
the backing fabric up the sides. Slip in
the battens at top and bottom.

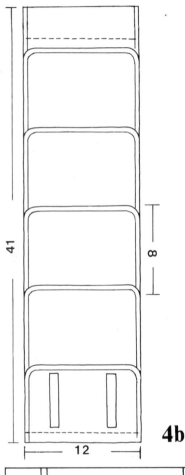

4b

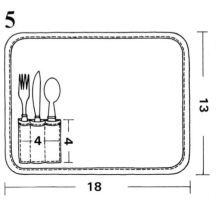

4a

PLACE MAT
Finished size 45 × 33cm (18 × 13in)

Materials needed for one mat
Cotton fabric: one piece 45 × 33cm
*   (18 × 13in); a pocket piece 12cm*
*   (5in) square*
Lining fabric: two pieces as above
Edge binding

Pin the cotton fabric and lining
oblongs together *wrong* sides facing.
Use a cup and chalk pencil to mark the
rounded corners. Then sew the pieces
together 1cm (½in) in from the edge all
around and trim the rounded corners.
Edge with binding.

To make the pocket, pin and tack
the cotton fabric and lining *right* sides
facing, then sew together allowing a
1cm (½in) seam and leaving a gap for
turning. Turn the pocket right side out
and sew closed the opening. Press well,
bind one edge then sew to the mat to
make the three pockets shown in **Fig 5**.

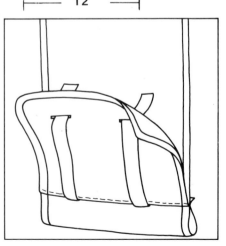

5

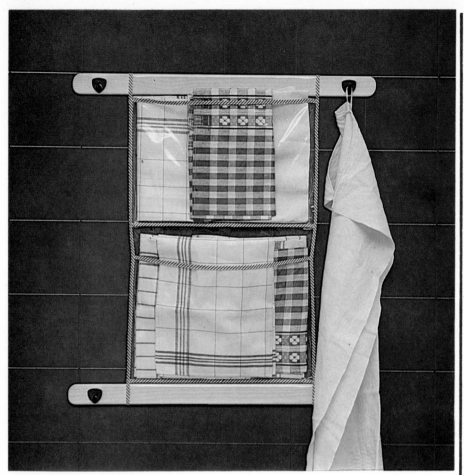

TABLE CLOTH POCKETS

Materials needed
*Cotton fabric for making under cloth
    and napkin pockets
Cotton fabric in complimentary color
    for over cloth*

This kind of combination makes a
pretty table setting with convenient
pockets in the over cloth to hold
napkins.

Measure your table and make up an
under cloth to fit. This consists of a

TEA TOWEL HOLDER
Finished size 67 × 40cm (26 × 16in)

Materials needed
*Clear plastic one piece 82 × 40cm
    (32 × 16in); two pocket pieces
    26 × 41cm (10 × 16½in)
Edge binding
Wooden batten: two pieces 4 × 1cm
    (1½ × ½in), and 64cm (25in) long
Four stick-on kitchen hooks
Polyurethane varnish*

Take the two pocket pieces and trim
the short edges so that they taper from
41cm (16½in) at the top down to 40cm
(16in) (i.e. the width of the tidy) at the
bottom. This allows a little extra room
at the mouth of each pocket.

Bind the top and bottom edges of
each pocket and pin to the large piece
of plastic 6cm (2½in) apart and about
12cm (5in) from either end. Sew the
pockets in position then bind the sides
of the tidy.

Turn over and stitch a hem at the
top and bottom of the plastic backing
to take the battens, and trim away any
excess plastic from the seam.

Round the ends of the battens and
give them a few coats of polyurethane
varnish. Slip the battens into the top
and bottom hems then stick on the
kitchen hooks to take the tea towels
that are in use (**Fig 6**).

6

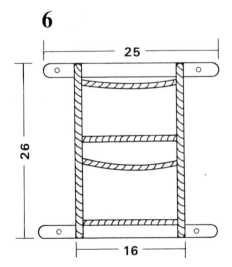

BOTTLE POCKETS

Materials needed
*Cotton fabric for backing piece, pocket
    band and two pocket bases
Iron-on stiffening for the fabric pieces
Edge binding
Wooden batten: one piece 6 × 1cm
    (2 × ½in) times width of tidy; one piece
    2.5 × 1cm (1 × ½in) times width of
    tidy.*

*We used ordinary cotton gingham for
this tidy, and to give it extra body and
strength backed it with iron-on stiffener.*

The double pocket is made from an
oblong band sewn round two pocket
bases. To measure the size of the
pocket band lay your bottles side by
side with about 2 × 3cm (1-1½in)
between them and measure the distance
XY (**Fig 8a**). The depth of the band
needs to be the bottle shoulder height
plus 2cm (¾in). Cut two heel-shaped
pocket bases (**Fig 8a**) allowing for a
1cm (½in) seam. Also cut a backing
piece the width PQ plus a suitable
length to allow for a top hem to take

gathered flounce that drops from the table top edge to the floor, attached to a piece that covers the table top (**Fig 7**). As a rough guide you will need a length of fabric about twice the circumference of the table for the gathered flounce.

Make up a square over cloth in the contrasting fabric and add a pocket in each corner made from the under cloth fabric.

7

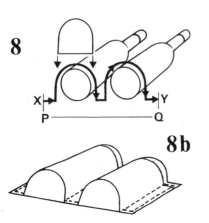

the 6cm (2in) batten and a bottom hem for the 2.5cm (1in) piece. Iron on the stiffener to all the fabric pieces.

Bind one long edge of the pocket band then firmly sew in the bases to the other long edge. Clip the two curves then sew the lower edge of the pocket band (now consisting of both band and the straight base edges) to the backing. Leave enough backing below this seam to make the lower batten hem.

Place the pockets on the backing and sew in position as in **Fig 8b**. Bind the sides of the backing, then sew the hem top and bottom for the battens.

8

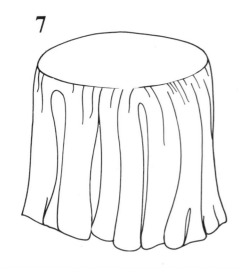

8b

WALL CASES

This is a marvelous way to display any of those little things that you find in your junk drawer during spring cleaning. If you are not going to throw them away, why not make the most of them? Three of these cases have been designed to look like partitioned drawers. You can make the partitions whatever size you like, to suit your collection.

For variation we have added a couple of fun ways to make cases without the carpentry–one is a jolly truck with cardboard boxes to carry toys; and the other is an extra-extra cheap case made only of cardboard and foil trays!

General note

There is nothing complicated about making the cases, but if you want to be proud of a professional-looking piece of handiwork you do need to measure and cut the wood accurately. To do this you will find a mitre box and tenon saw invaluable.

KITCHEN CASES

Finished size of the pair 55 × 51cm (22 × 20in)

Materials needed for each case

Wood: 1.60m (5ft) of 1.5 × 6.5cm ($\frac{1}{2}$ × $2\frac{1}{2}$in) wide section (two pieces 51cm (20in) long; two pieces 24cm ($9\frac{1}{2}$in) long)
Wood for partitions 1 × 4.5cm ($\frac{3}{8}$ × $1\frac{3}{4}$in) wide; 1.25m (4ft) for left hand case; 1.70m ($5\frac{1}{2}$ft) for right (20 × $11\frac{1}{2}$in)
Plywood for backing: 51 × 27cm (20 × $11\frac{1}{2}$in); 6mm ($\frac{1}{4}$in) thick
Brass fittings: four corner and two mounting brackets with screws; one brass handle
Wood stain and varnish

If you have a shallow drawer you could convert by partitioning then so much the better, but if not then make up a couple from scratch as we did and add all the authentic fittings!

Make up two frames using the 1.5 × 6.5cm ($\frac{1}{2}$ × $2\frac{1}{2}$in) wood. Abut the ends and glue and pin them. Then glue and pin on the plywood backing.

To make the partitions (**Fig 1**) cut the 1 × 4.5cm ($\frac{3}{8}$ × $1\frac{3}{4}$in) wood into sections and secure each partition piece in position by gluing and pinning through from the back of the plywood.

Sand the frame well and apply the stain. Then finish with a couple of coats of polyurethane varnish and add the corner brackets, handles and mountings.

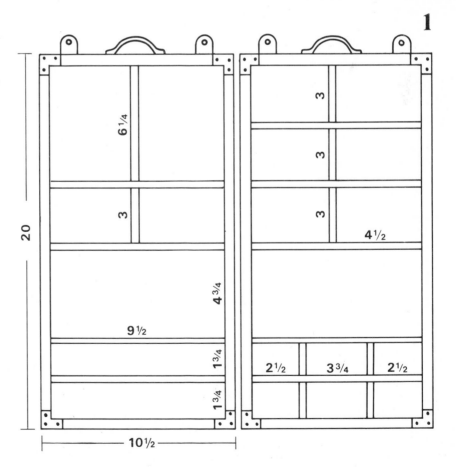

FOIL CASE
Finished size 60 × 40cm (24 × 16in)

Materials needed
Wooden batten: one piece 6 × 1cm
(2½ × ½in) wide, 38cm (15in) long
Thick cardboard or 3mm (⅛in) plywood,
40 × 60cm (16 × 24in)
Foil trays
Paint

This is one way of making a very
inexpensive display case–just use the
kind of foil food trays sold in freezer
stores.

Round the edges of the plywood or
cardboard using a plate as a guide.
Then stick the wooden batten across
the lower edge at the back. This will act
as a spacer between the wall and the
board making sure the sloping sides of
the trays make level ledges.

Paint the board, stick on the trays
then drill two holes in the top of the
board to fix it to the wall.

THE PIGEONHOLE CASE
Finished size 83 × 42cm (33 × 16½in)

Materials needed
Wooden batten: 9.50m (31ft) of
3.5cm × 6mm (1½ × ¼in)
Plywood: one piece 6mm (¼in) thick,
83 × 42cm (33 × 16½in)
Two mounting brackets
Wood primer and spray paint

Make up a frame 83 × 42cm
(33 × 16½in) in size using the batten.
Abut the ends and glue and pin the
corners. Then glue and pin the
plywood on the back of the frame.

Cut and fix the main partition pieces,
i.e. those that divide the case into eight
equal size compartments (**Fig 2**). Fix
the three vertical ones first then the
main cross one. You can make the
pigeonholes any size to suit your own
taste and requirements.

Sand the case, prime it and then
paint using the spray paint—this is
very much less laborious than painting
with a brush. When dry fix the
mountings and fill the case with your
favorite knick-knacks.

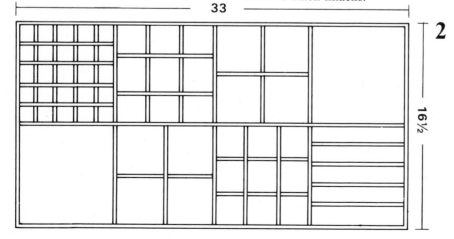

33

16½

2

GLASSED CASE

Finished size 51 × 37.5cm (20½ × 15¼in)

Materials needed

Wooden batten for main frame: one
1.5 × 6cm (¾ × 2½in) piece, 51cm long
(20½in); two 1 × 6cm (½ × 2½in)
pieces 35cm (14in) long, one piece
51cm (20½in) long

Wooden batten for partitions: 3m (10ft)
of 4.5 × 1cm (1¾ × ½in) section

Wooden molding to hold glass: 1.7m of
1 × 1cm (⅜ × ⅜in) section

Plywood: one 6mm (¼in) thick piece
37.5 × 51cm (15¼ × 20½in)

Glass: one 3mm (⅛in) thick piece
34.5 × 48.5cm (13¾ × 19¼in)

Brass fittings: four flat angle brackets
1cm (½in) wide; two mounting
brackets

Two decorative handles

Wood stain, mat varnish

Like the Kitchen Cases this too can
actually be a converted drawer or just
made to look like one.

Use the 1cm (½in) thick batten to
make up three sides of the main frame.
Use the 1.5cm (¾in) thick piece at the
top of the frame to make what would
be the front of the drawer. Abut the
ends of the pieces and glue and pin the
corners. Then glue and pin the piece of
plywood on the back of the frame.

Cut and fix the four 35cm (14in) long
vertical partitions (**Fig 3**). Secure them
by gluing, and pinning through the
back of the plywood. Then cut and fit
one complete diagonal length in the
centre section. Lay the other diagonal
length in position then mark and cut
where it crosses the first diagonal.
Similarly mark and cut a length to
make the two cross pieces in this
section. Fix all these pieces in place
along with the horizontal partitions in
the end compartments.

To hold the glass in place cut four
lengths of the 1cm (⅜in) molding to
make an inner frame with abutted
corners (see photograph). Stain and
mat varnish these lengths plus the rest
of the case, then add the brass fittings
and handles.

Fill the case with dried flowers and
plastic fruit (these need to be stuck or
pinned to the case), put in the glass and
hold in place with the molding tacked
to the side of the case.

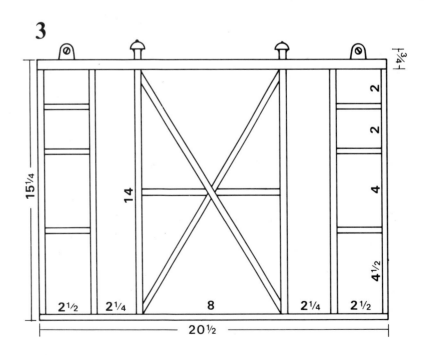

3

READYMADE CASE

Here's just an idea for a readymade case. These types of molded plastic trays with lots of compartments are sometimes sold in tool shops as storage trays for nails and screws etc. If you can get one in a bright color they make ideal display cases. Alternatively you could buy cutlery trays. To hang, drill a small hole in each of the upper corners to take screws, nails or hooks.

TRUCK

Finished size 110 × 100cm (44 × 40in)

Materials needed

Plywood one 1cm ($\frac{1}{2}$in) thick piece
   110 × 100cm (44 × 40in)
Various strong cardboard boxes
Enamel paints
Adhesive; sticky brown paper tape

Our jolly truck design is shown in **Fig 4**. Draw up the pattern to size on the plywood then cut out the shape using a coping saw. Sand the edges smooth. Drill two holes at the top for hanging.

Paint the various parts of the truck in cheerful colors (see photograh). The small tins of enamel paint sold for model-making are probably the most economical way of buying lots of colors in small quantities.

Use the sticky brown paper tape to strengthen and tidy up the edges of the cardboard boxes, then paint them too. You may find that the cardboard will soak up the paint so a couple of coats will probably be needed–in fact this will help to strengthen the cardboard.

Stick the boxes on with adhesive.

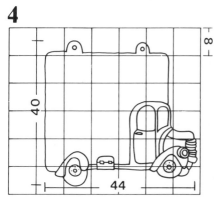

4

TYPECASE
Finished size 85 × 58cm (33½ × 22½in)

Materials needed

*Wooden batten for frame and main
partitions: 4.5m (15ft) of 1.5 × 6cm
(½ × 2½in) section (two pieces 84.5cm
(33½in) long, three pieces 55cm
(21½in) long, 2 pieces 40cm (16in)
long)*

*Wooden batten for minor partitions: 7m
(23ft) of 1 × 4.5cm (⅜ × 1¾in) section*

*Plywood: one 6mm (¼in) thick piece
84.5 × 58cm (33½ × 22½in)*

*Brass fittings: two mountings; two
handles (optional)*

Wood stain

Mat varnish

This design is based on the kind of case
that printers use to keep their metal
type in. Make up the frame, back it
with the plywood and add the main
partitions as for all the previous
wooden cases. Then add the minor
partitions **Fig 5**.

Sand the case well then dab on the
stain with a piece of cloth so that it is
unevenly absorbed by the wood. This
will give the whole case a kind of
antique finish. Give the case a couple
of coats of mat varnish then fix on the
mountings plus a handle at either end if
you like.

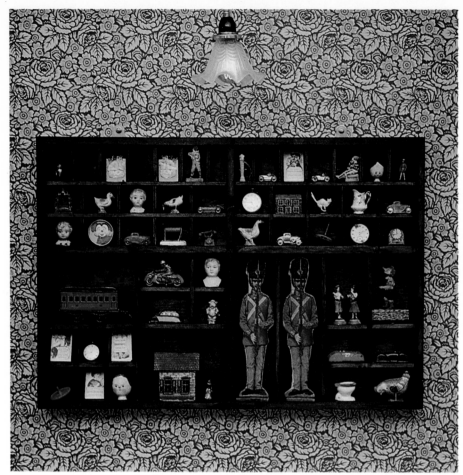

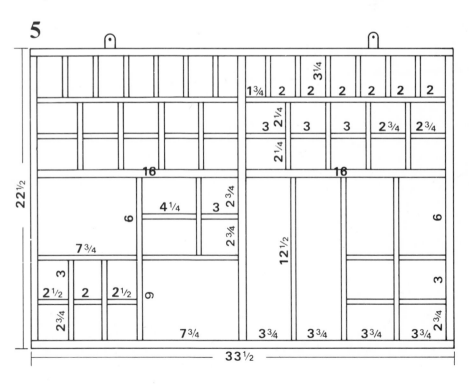

5

BRIGHT BAGS

Here are several fun ideas for carryalls. Some you carry, some you actually strap on leaving your arms completely free! These ones make excellent school bags or play carryalls for children but remember that children come in different sizes, so measure yours first and adjust the measurements accordingly. The basic designs are all simple—just adapt the pocket arrangements to suit your own needs.

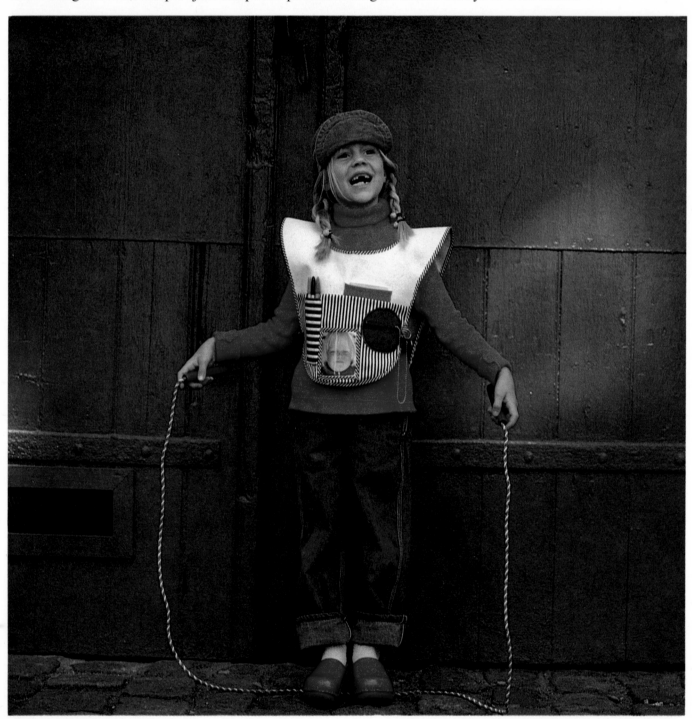

General note

For all the bags we used a tough thick cotton–canvas or denim is ideal. Most raw edges are finished with a complimentary binding, and the closures for the pockets are either zippers or simple button fastenings. It is a good idea to use a double ring or a prongless buckle fastening on all the straps so that you don't have to bother with eyelets. The straps themselves can be made up in your cotton fabric, or easier still, just buy some tough webbing in a matching color–carpet bindings are ideal and come in a range of colors.

JERKIN CARRYALL

For the main jerkin piece cut a piece of tough cotton the shape and size shown in **Fig 1a** (the wider end makes the back of the jerkin). Cut a piece of fabric to make up the major front pocket (i.e. the big striped one in the photograph) and to it add some other smaller pockets (**Fig 1b**)–we made one of these in clear plastic as a 'picture' pocket. Then stitch the main pocket to the tunic front.

Cut the fabric for the big buttoned pocket on the back (**Fig 1c** and photograph) and to it stitch the zippered stripy pocket. Make the buttonhole in the main pocket then stitch the pocket to the jerkin back and sew on a button.

Finish all the raw edges with seam binding and finally sew on pairs of straps to fasten the jerkin sides.

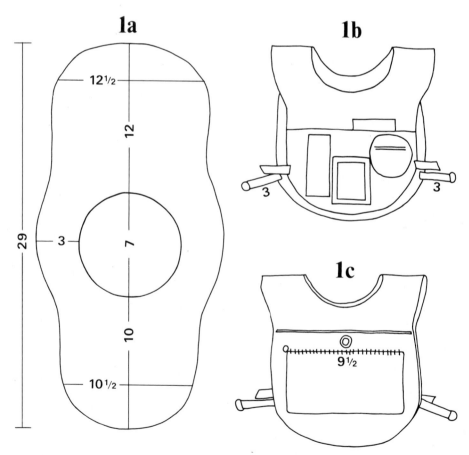

155

TANK TOP CARRYALL

Cut the main part in one by placing the 20cm (8in) side on a fold (**Fig 2a**). Alternatively if your fabric isn't wide enough cut two pieces and join them along this 20cm (8in) side.

The main zippered pockets on back and front (see photographs) are identical except for the smaller pockets added to them (**Fig 2b** shows the finished details of these two main pockets). For each main pocket cut a square of fabric plus a long strip to go all around as a gusset–allow 1cm ($\frac{1}{2}$in) extra all around for seams. In the middle of each long strip sew in a zipper, then sew the ends of the gusset strip together–note that when the pocket is assembled this join will lie to the bottom of the pocket.

Add the extra pockets to the square pocket pieces e.g. the round one with slit opening to the front piece and a square one divided to make a double pocket to the back. Then sew these pocket squares into the zippered gussets (right sides facing) rounding the corners. Trim and clip the corners.

Now pin and tack these zippered pockets to back and front of the tank top turning under your seam allowance and neatly sewing close to the pocket edges.

Stitch the tunic together along the shoulders (right sides facing) sloping the seams to fit the wearer's shoulders (**Fig 2c**). Trim off the excess fabric. Stitch on loops and buttons to make the side closure then finish all remaining raw edges with binding.

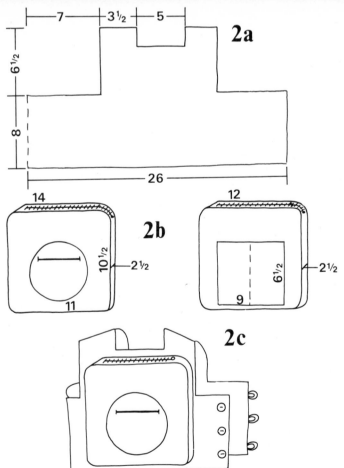

FLORAL RUCKSACK

In good tough fabric cut one of piece X (the front of the bag) and one of piece Y (the back) allowing an extra 1cm (½in) on the seams. The dots at the top of piece X in **Fig 3a** indicate the eyelet positions for a draw-string tie that gathers the top of the bag and is hidden under the buttoned flap.

Turn over a hem along the eyelet edge on piece X and fix in several eyelets (sets of these can be bought from most large haberdashery stores). To piece Y add the shoulder straps (**Fig 3b–Fig 3c** gives the strap lengths). Then sew together X and Y to make the basic bag.

For the flap cut two of piece Z (allowing an extra 1cm (½in) all around) and sew together right sides facing around the curved edge. Turn right side out, press and finish the curved edge with a line of stitching. Add a 'picture' pocket (see **Fig 3d** and photograph) to the flap if you like, then sew the flap to the back of the bag. Make a button hole in the flap and sew on a button. Finally thread a cord drawstring through the eyelets.

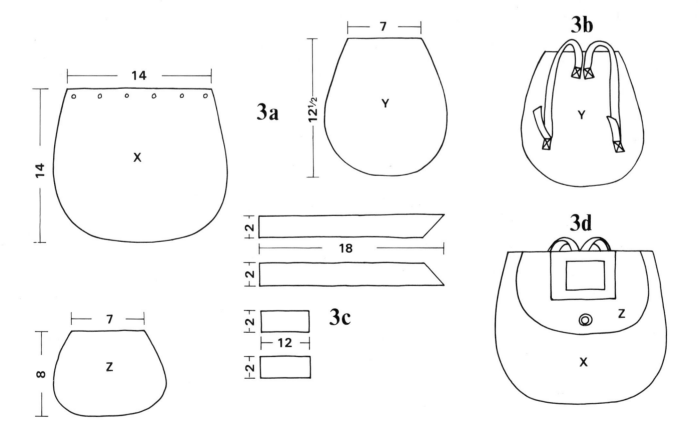

STRIPY RUCKSACK

This bag basically consists of two squarish fabric pieces X (**Fig 4a**) making the back and front of the bag, joined by a gusset strip Y which takes a zipper.

Cut two X pieces and one of Y allowing 1cm ($\frac{1}{2}$in) all around for the seams. Insert the zipper in the middle of the gusset strip and sew together the short edges of the strip. Along the section that will make the side of the rucksack stitch on a pocket the same width as the gusset.

To one of the square fabric pieces add the round and the large oblong pocket, then sew the square piece into the gusset (**Fig 4b**).

Sew on the shoulder straps (**Fig 4a** indicates the sizes) to the other square fabric piece then sew this into the gusset, right sides together. Turn the bag right side out through the zipper opening **Fig 4c**.

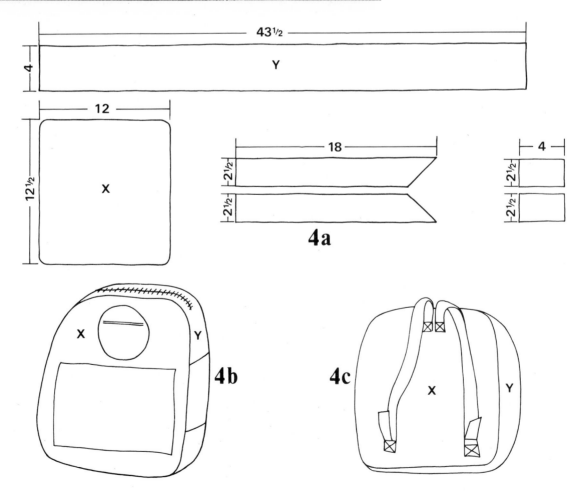

DUAL PURPOSE BAG

To make the two main parts of the bag cut four of piece X (**Fig 5a**) allowing 1cm ($\frac{1}{2}$in) all around for the seam. Sew these together in pairs right sides facing leaving a gap for turning. Turn right side out, stitch the gap closed, press well and finish each panel with a line of stitching around the edge.

To one of these panels add the front pockets PQRS as in **Fig 5b** (**Fig 5a** gives the sizes) or any other arrangement you prefer. To the other panel add the zippered pocket T and the pair of magazine straps (**Fig 5c**). To finish, add the shoulder straps and side straps.

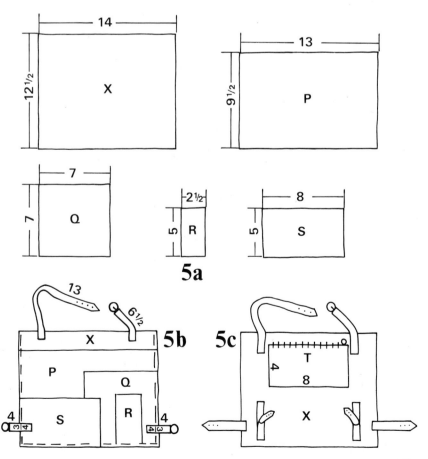

BLACK STUDIO BAG

First make up the bag flap. Cut two of piece Z (**Fig 6a**), one in tough cotton fabric, the other in lining fabric. Allow an extra 1cm ($\frac{1}{2}$in) all around for the seam. Sew the two pieces together, right sides facing, leaving a gap for turning. Turn right side out and stitch the gap closed. Press the edges well and make them neat with a line of stitching all around. Add a pocket to the flap if you like (see photograph).

To make the main part of the bag, cut one of piece X in the tough cotton, adding on a 1cm ($\frac{1}{2}$in) seam allowance all around. Cut two of pieces Y in the cotton, allowing an extra 1cm ($\frac{1}{2}$in) all around for the seam.

Sew on some pockets to piece X and bind the edges of the cutouts. Then take each Y piece and sew a small hem on one end. (The hems will make the top edges of the bag sides.)

Sew the Y pieces into the main part of the bag, right sides facing. Then turn over and stitch the hems at the top of the bag to take the two 40cm × 12mm ($16 \times \frac{1}{2}$in) dowel handles. Also stitch on the edge of the flap at the base of one of the hems (**Fig 6b**).

To strengthen the bottom of the bag, cut a piece of cardboard W (**Fig 6a**) to fit, cover it with fabric and glue to the bottom of the bag inside.

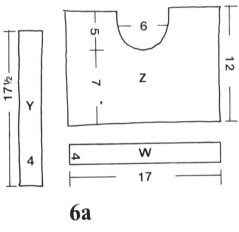

6a

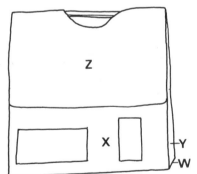

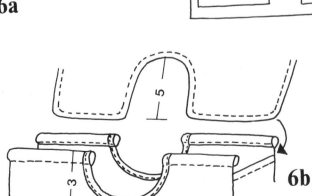

6b

DENIM SLING BAG

This simple sling holder, rather like a pair of saddle bags is especially cheap to make if you have any old denim clothes in the rag bag.

Fig 7a shows the main pattern piece to cut, but if you don't have the length of fabric to cut it in one, make it up in two pieces joined in the middle. Also cut or make up a similar piece in lining fabric. Sew the two pieces together right sides facing and turn right side out. Press well and run a couple of lines of stitching around the edges to neaten.

Then just add pockets–some of these can be salvaged ready made from old clothes. The pocket arrangement we used is shown in **Fig 7b** and the photographs–pocket X is simply a side pocket cut from a pair of jeans.

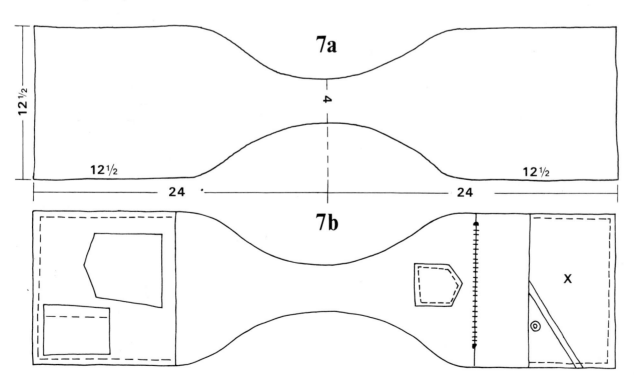

Display boards really are indispensable, as you'll find once you've made some of these. They are every bit as useful in the home as they are in the office, and they can look good too. If you're a hoarder of postcards or clippings, always have to fumble in drawers for address cards, or never know where the key to the garden shed is, then get them all up on a board!

We have designed several different ones here, some for general use so that you can keep a constant collage going, and some with a specific purpose, like the key board and the kitchen board. For those who make a hobby of collecting postcards, we have dreamed up a board that looks just like a giant postcard. So have fun using your imagination for your own types of display board!

FOLD AWAY TABLE BOARD

Materials needed

Pine wood: 2.2 × 5.6cm (1 × 2¼in) thick–six pieces 81cm long (31¾in); six pieces 62.8cm long (25¼in)
Wooden molding: 8.25m (27ft) of 1cm (½in) square section
Insulation board: two 12mm (½in) thick pieces 69.5 × 62.5cm (27 × 25in)
Blockboard: one 12mm (½in) thick piece 69.5 × 62.5 (27 × 25in)
Dowel to make joining pegs approx. 5mm (¼in)
Hinges: four 7cm (3in)
Wood adhesive; panel pins; two strong screw eye hooks

Make up three frames using the 5.6mm (2¼in) wide wood (**Fig 1a**).

Abut the corners to make 81 × 74cm frames (31¾ × 29¾in). Join the corners by the dowelling joint method explained in Hints. Then cut lengths of the 1cm (½in) molding to make up three inner frames (**Fig 1b**). Stick and pin the molding flush with one surface on the large frame leaving a 12mm (½in) recess to take the board. Varnish the frames.

Cover the two insulation boards with hemp cloth and fit each one into a frame by gluing and pinning through the back of the board into the inner frame.

To make the table section paint or varnish the blockboard then glue and pin into the third frame. Note that unlike the display boards the 1cm (½in) inner frame here makes the back of the frame i.e. a ledge for the table top to sit on.

Fix the three boards together so that they can hinge as shown in **Fig 1c**. Put two strong screw eye hooks in the top of the upper notice board and fix it firmly to the wall at an appropriate height with screws through the hooks.

To hold the boards up in their folded position make the little fitting shown in **Fig 1d** from two pieces of dowel. This diagram also shows the folded profile of the boards plus the hinge positions.

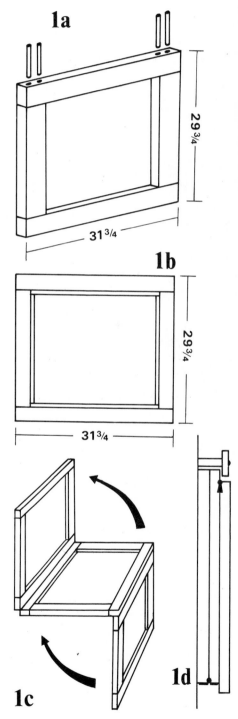

1a

29¾

31¾

1b

29¾

31¾

1c

1d

POSTCARD BOARD

Materials needed

Plywood: one 4mm ($\frac{1}{4}$in) piece
102 × 55cm (40 × 22in)
Wooden molding 2.2cm (1in) square;
two pieces 102cm (40in) long, three
pieces 50.5cm (20in) long
Insulation board: one 12mm ($\frac{1}{2}$in) thick
piece 60 × 50.5cm (24 × 20in)
Blackboard paint; black and white gloss
paint
Wood adhesive; panel pins
Black felt to cover board

Stick the 2.2cm (1in) molding to the
plywood as in **Fig 3** to make two
compartments. Pin through into the
molding from the back of the plywood
to secure the frame firmly. Paint the
frame pieces glossy black and give the
address compartment a coat of the
blackboard paint. When everything is
dry add the white dividing line and the
four address lines that you usually see
on postcards. Mask either side of the
lines with masking tape before you
paint–this will ensure a neat straight
line–or alternatively make the lines

KEY BOARD

Materials needed

Plywood: one 4mm ($\frac{1}{4}$in) thick piece,
30 × 60cm (12 × 24in)
Wooden molding 1.6cm ($\frac{3}{4}$in) square
section: two pieces 60cm; two pieces
30cm (12in)
Half-round wooden molding 2.2cm
(1in) section, 27cm (10$\frac{1}{2}$in) long
Dowel: one piece 2.2cm (1in) diameter,
35cm (15in) long
5 small screw-in hooks; 10 screw eye
hooks (with large eyes); 5 small key
rings
Wood adhesive, paints, polyurethane
varnish, panel pins

Mitre the corners of the 1.6cm ($\frac{3}{4}$in)
square molding and stick around the
edge of the plywood to make a frame.
Pin through from the back of the
plywood to secure the frame. Draw
and paint the keyhole motif on the
plywood (see **Fig 2**). Sand the ends of
the half-round molding so it fits neatly
within the width of the frame and stick
in position (**Fig 2**). Give the whole
frame a couple of coats of varnish then

screw in the small hooks to the half-
round molding.

Cut the dowel into five 7cm (3in)
lengths (sand the ends well) and paint
them different colors so you can easily
identify each key. Fix a screw eye hook
in each end of these colored 'holders',
hang the holders on the board and the
key rings on the ends of the holders.

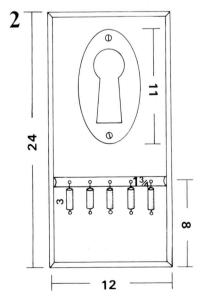

BRASS-BOUND BOARD

Materials needed

Wood and board as for display board
section of Fold Away Table Board
Piece of tartan fabric to cover board
Four brass corner fittings
Wood stain and varnish

This is just a variation on the original
display board for the Fold Away Table
Board described on page 163. It is
made in exactly the same way and
merely hung the other way up (**Fig 4**).
To give this board its totally different
character just stain the wood before
varnishing, add some decorative brass
corner fittings, and use a dark tartan
over the board.

with some narrow adhesive tape.

Cover the insulation board with black felt then press into the frame. All you have to do now is wait for the postcards to arrive!

3

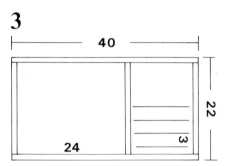

4

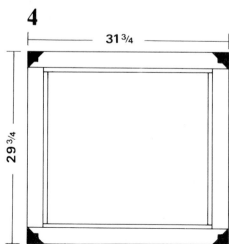

PICTURE FRAME BOARD

This is definitely the quickest and easiest notice board to make–that is if you have a large old frame handy! Just paint the frame, cut a piece of insulation board to size, cover it with fabric and fit into the frame. Attach the board in the back of the frame with a few tacks.

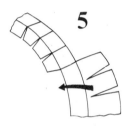

5

CIRCULAR BOARD

Materials needed
Insulation board: one piece 100cm (40in) square
Felt: one piece 110 (44in) square
Adhesive

Draw in diagonals across the board to find the center. Fasten one end of a piece of string to the centre with a drawing pin then tie a pencil to the other end so that you can draw a circle that comes just within the edges of the board.

Cut out the circle using a coping saw. Spread adhesive over the front of the board, cover with the felt and smooth it down well. Trim the felt to make a circle roughly 5cm (2in) larger than the board. Then cut V's in the felt edge all the way around to make small flaps that can be neatly folded around the edge of the board and stuck to the back with adhesive (**Fig 5**). You could use a staple gun instead.

KITCHEN BOARD
Finished size 84 × 56cm (34 × 23in)

Materials needed
Wood: one piece 2.2cm (1in) thick,
12 × 56.5cm (5 × 23in)
Wooden molding: 2.2cm (1in) square:
two pieces 72cm (29in) long; one
piece 52cm (21in) long
Wooden molding 1cm (½in) square: one
piece 56.5cm (23in) long
Insulation board: one piece 12mm (½in)
thick, 67.5 × 52cm (27 × 21in)
Clear plastic: one thick sheet
72 × 56.5cm (29 × 23in)
Wood stain and varnish
Wood adhesive; panel pins; screws

We simply adapted a chopping board design to give this board its kitchen flavor–the plastic overlay keeps your pictures and recipes from getting greasy.

Make up a frame using the four pieces of 2.2cm (1in) molding. Pin the corners and use adhesive on the abutted edges. From the piece of 12 × 56.5cm (5 × 23in) wood cut the handle shape shown in **Fig 6a.** Use a padsaw or coping saw to make the cuts and smooth the edges well with sandpaper. Fix the handle piece on the top of the frame using adhesive along the join and also screw through from the inside of the frame with countersunk screws. Darken the whole frame with a stain and give it a couple of coats of varnish–or you can use a colored polyurethane varnish.

Check that the board is an exact fit for the frame then spread adhesive on the board edges and along the inside of the frame. Press the board into the frame and secure by pinning through the edges of the frame. (The board can be painted or covered with colored paper before fitting it in the frame.)

Fix the 1cm (½in) molding over the board with tacks to hold one end of the plastic sheet (**Fig 6b**). This molding should just cover the join between the top of the frame and the handle section.

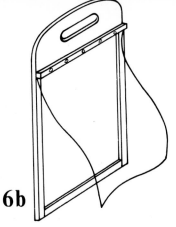

6a **6b**

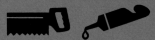

Cork is such an attractive material, and so easy to work with that we think it deserves a far wider use than just on walls and floors. So here is a whole range of ideas which you can copy, adapt, or which may inspire you to find exciting new applications for cork.

General note
Everything in this section needs cork tiles for covering. You will also need contact glue for gluing wood and cork surfaces and some clear polyurethane varnish to give the cork and wood a durable finish–the cork may require an extra coat or two, as it tends to absorb the varnish.

Tiles can be cut easily and accurately with a craft knife against a steel rule. The lengths of wooden edging batten are all cut at 45°, and the best way to do this is to use a mitre box.

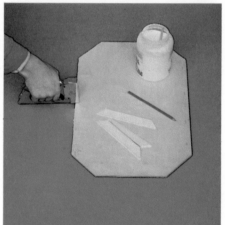

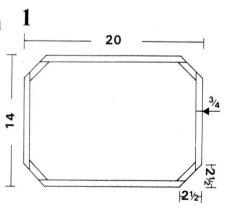

SUPPER BOARD
Materials needed
Plywood: 4mm ($\frac{1}{4}$in) thick; piece
*   50 × 35cm (20 × 14in)*
Wooden batten: 1.8m–19 × 6mm
*   (6ft–$\frac{3}{4}$ × $\frac{1}{4}$in) cross section*

Cut 6cm (2$\frac{1}{2}$in) corners off the plywood
to make it the shape shown in **Fig 1**.
Next cut lengths of batten to fit around
the surface edge of the tray as shown in
Fig 1. Glue the lengths of edging
around the board flush with the edge,
then weight them until the glue dries.
Staple through from the back too if
you like (see photograph).

Sand the whole frame to give a good
finish. Cut the cork tiles to fit the board
within the edging and glue them into
position (see photograph). Then
varnish all surfaces.

1

20

14

3/4

2½

2½

TRAY
Materials needed
Plywood: 4mm ($\frac{1}{4}$in); piece 50 × 35cm
*   *(20 × 14in)*
Wooden batten: piece 2m–19 × 6mm
*   *(7ft–$\frac{3}{4}$ × $\frac{1}{4}$in) cross-section;*
*   *piece 2m–42 × 12mm (7ft–1$\frac{1}{2}$ × $\frac{1}{2}$in)*
*   *cross-section*

Cut the plywood as for the Supper
Board. Then cut the 42mm (1$\frac{1}{8}$in)
batten into mitred lengths and glue
into position to make the tray edge
(**Fig 2**). Pin through the plywood into
the bottom of the batten to make the
edges really firm.

Cover the tray center and edges with
cork then cap the edge with the 19mm
batten. Apply varnish.

If you have an old tray you could
simply cover it with cork tiles and then
varnish.

DISPLAY BOARD
Materials needed
Plywood: 4mm ($\frac{1}{4}$in) thick; piece
*   *65 × 52cm (26 × 21in)*
Wooden batten: 3.8–19 × 6mm
*   *(12$\frac{1}{2}$ft–$\frac{3}{4}$ × $\frac{1}{4}$in) cross-section*
Picture glass: 34 × 25cm (13$\frac{1}{2}$ × 10in)
*   *(i.e. inner dimensions of center*
*   *frame)*

Cut 10cm (4in) corners off the plywood
to reduce it to the shape shown in
Fig 3. Cut and stick on the edging
batten (as for Supper Board) plus the
cork. Make up the inner frame (**Fig 3**)
as accurately as you can, glue in place
and also pin it through from the
underside of the board.

PICTURE FRAME
Make up in exactly the same way as the
Display Board, but you will need in
addition a piece of picture glass
34 × 25cm (13$\frac{1}{2}$ × 10in). Slip your
picture into the inner frame then press
the glass into the frame. (Obviously it

WRITING PAD
Materials needed
Plywood: 4mm ($\frac{1}{4}$in) thick; piece
*   *65 × 52cm (26 × 21in)*
Wooden batten: 2.4m–19 × 6mm
*   *(8ft–$\frac{3}{4}$ × $\frac{1}{4}$in) cross-section*

Make up exactly as for the Picture
Frame but without the inner frame. As
part of a desk set you could also make
a cork-covered pen holder along the
lines of the flower-pot holder in the
photograph on page 168. Or you could
cover a hinged wooden cigar box or
candy box and use it as a desk holder.

should be a fairly tight fit.) If it is
slightly loose, tap in a small picture
glazing brad on each side just to secure
the glass.

Fig 4 gives suitable dimensions for
similar smaller frames.

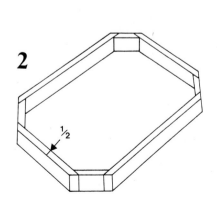

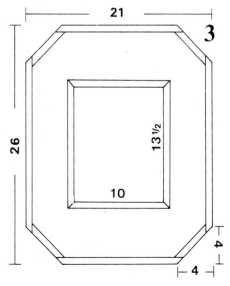

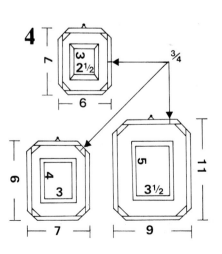

SCREEN
Materials needed
Chipboard: 12mm ($\frac{1}{2}$in) thick; 4 pieces
155 × 40cm (62 × 16in)
Wooden batten: 17m–19 × 6mm
(56ft–$\frac{3}{4}$ × $\frac{1}{4}$in) cross-section
6 brass hinges plus screws

The top and bottom of each panel in
this screen is cut away in a series of
5cm (2in) steps (see photograph and
Fig 5). Draw your cutting lines on each
piece of the chipboard in pencil, cut
out these profiles and sand smooth all
edges.

Cover both sides of the chipboard
panels with cork, then cut the
appropriate number of mitred batten
lengths needed to cover both the
stepped and straight edges. Glue and
pin the batten to cover the bare edges
of the screen.

Varnish the completed panels and
screw them together with the hinges.

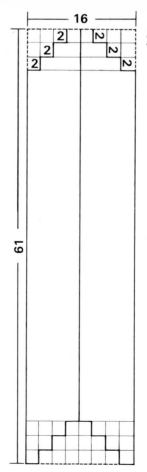

16

5

2 2
2 2
2 2

61

TABLE
Materials needed

Chipboard 19mm ($\frac{3}{4}$in) thick: piece
135 × 105cm (53 × 41in)
Chipboard 16mm ($\frac{5}{8}$in) thick: 4 pieces
70 × 45cm (28 × 18in)
Wooden batten: 5m–32 × 16mm
(16ft–1$\frac{1}{4}$ × $\frac{5}{8}$in) cross-section
Wooden batten: 2m–66 × 8mm
(7ft–2$\frac{1}{2}$ × $\frac{3}{8}$in) cross-section
Wooden batten: 1m–12 × 12mm
(40in × $\frac{1}{2}$ × $\frac{1}{2}$in) cross-section
Chipboard screws

Cut 25cm (10in) corners off the large piece of chipboard to reduce it to the size shown in **Fig 6**. Sand the edges smooth.

Next make the square table base using the four chipboard pieces. Abut the edges as in **Fig 7**, gluing and screwing the joints. Sand the edges smooth. Cover the base sides with cork, then use the 8mm ($\frac{3}{8}$in) batten to make the base edging (**Fig 8**).

To the underside of the table top glue and screw on two pieces of the 12 × 12mm ($\frac{1}{2}$ × $\frac{1}{2}$in) batten to fit snugly inside the top of the base. Then cover the table top with cork, trimming it flush with the edges of the chipboard. Cut mitred lengths of the 16mm ($\frac{5}{8}$in) batten for the edging and glue to the table edge so that the 16mm ($\frac{5}{8}$in) side is either flush with or just a little proud of the table surface.

Give all the cork and wood surfaces several coats of varnish and when dry place the table top on the base **Fig 9**.

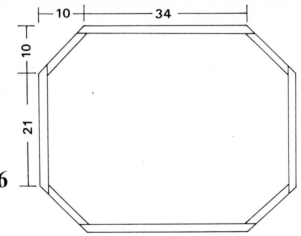

6

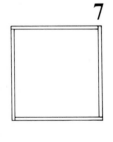

7

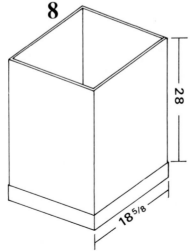

8

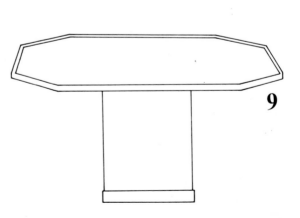

9